I0539157

Foreword by Rhonda Boyle

KEYS THAT FIT

MICHAEL TESSLER

How a Common-Sense Innovation Is
Transforming the Musical Lives of
Pianists Around the World

Published by Michael Tessler Photography LLC, publishing division
8545 W. Warm Springs Road
#A4-284
Las Vegas, NV 89113

Edited by Ellen Scholnicoff

Foreword by Rhonda Boyle

ISBN (Paperback): 979-8-218-76305-3
ASIN (eBook): B0FR3RRNRW

For all pianists who've ever wished for larger hands, and for those who tirelessly advocate for alternative keyboard sizes.

And for my parents who gave me two perfect hands and the common sense, courage, and determination to find a piano keyboard that fits them.

TABLE OF CONTENTS

|| |||

FOREWORD

For about 140 years, piano keys have been available in just one size – a size that best suits adult men with large hands. In the late 19th century, piano keys became wider as part of the redesign of the acoustic piano to suit large concert halls where large-handed male virtuosos performed. This 'one-size-fits-all' keyboard was effectively 'locked in' by industrialisation. Before then, all pianists were playing pianos with keyboards narrower than today's conventional size. Although women played in large numbers, social conventions of the time meant that they were essentially restricted to teaching and performing in the home.

With the standardisation of 'wide' keys, most women, children as well as smaller-handed men face a significant disadvantage with a keyboard that does not suit their hands. In fact, research shows that the conventional keyboard is too large for 87% of adult females and 24% of adult males. More than half of all pianists playing or aspiring to play at an advanced level would label themselves as 'small-handed' and wish that they had larger hands.

The pattern of concert platforms and elite competition winners being male dominated still prevails to this day, not so much due to direct discrimination but indirectly because the conventional keyboard locks out or restricts so many from reaching their potential. Bizarrely, delegates at piano pedagogy conferences around the world today are mostly women, where they enjoy special performances by famous large-handed male artists, often competition winners, who play repertoire that most delegates could not play, or only with pain, discomfort or compromised musicality.

For over a decade, I have been receiving emails and messages from hundreds of pianists around the world who want a change to the lack of choice of key width. Many who signed a worldwide petition have left heartfelt comments. They consistently refer to their desperation at not being able to play the pieces they love, and the despair caused by pain and injury that has often ended careers. Those who do try narrow keys often talk about the 'revelation' they experience. The emotions they feel include joy at being able to play pieces they have always had to avoid, to play without pain, as well as anger at the countless hours of wasted time as they realise that their lack of talent or application was not the problem – it was a keyboard that was way too big for their hands.

A small number of well-known professional pianists or relatively wealthy amateurs have been and still are able to have special pianos or retrofitted keyboards with narrow keys made for them by high-end acoustic manufacturers and speciality keyboard makers. Over the last two decades, narrow keys have become more widespread and better known, starting with the original vision of Chris Donison and David Steinbuhler in the 1990s. Since then, through the continued dedication of David Steinbuhler who established the non-profit DS Standard Foundation in 2018, DS® keyboards have been installed in more than 20 music schools and universities in North America, and many more in teaching studios and private homes around the world.

Michael Tessler's innovative Kaduk digital piano has an octave almost one and a half inches less than the conventional piano keyboard. This allows him to not only reach an octave very comfortably but play any tenths. For the first time in his life, he is fulfilling his dream of being able to play the works of Oscar Peterson as intended by that great jazz pianist of the 20th century. His book eloquently expresses the emotions he encountered in his journey to pianistic freedom and the immense satisfaction and joy he now experiences on this piano. While his story will be of particular interest to jazz pianists, it will resonate with all pianists. His book is a valuable contribution to the cause of encouraging manufacturers to make narrow keys widely available, in both acoustic and digital pianos, as mainstream options to all. This paradigm change will revolutionise and reinvigorate the industry and change the lives of millions of pianists around the world.

Rhonda Boyle

Global Coordinator, Pianists for Alternatively Sized Keyboards (PASK)
Board member, DS Standard Foundation Inc
International Liaison, Stretto Piano Concerts

INTRODUCTION

Imagine living in a world in which all printed materials use such small font that only individuals with the most exceptional eyesight are able to read them. Others can make out some of the words or even complete sentences here and there, but only the lucky folks with "super vision" are able to reap the full benefit of all the reading material out there. Because paper and ink are so expensive in this society, printing houses make the text as small as possible—a size that suits anyone with super vision.

Even though most people do not have super vision and struggle with the tiny print, the convention becomes so deeply ingrained that the obvious solution—printing larger books with larger text—is dismissed as too costly, impractical, and unnecessary. Some people without super vision shy away from the idea of using larger print out of fear that they will be considered weak for needing this adaptation. As a result, most readers end up straining their eyes to read, making reading much less enjoyable for them than it should be. They read for shorter periods of time and choose different reading materials to accommodate their "handicap", such as picture books, further limiting their enjoyment. Some of them stop reading altogether.

Sounds like the setting for a dystopian work of fiction, doesn't it? Yet this imaginary world is surprisingly similar to the reality smaller-handed pianists have been facing for years. A long time ago, the familiar piano keyboard most of us use today was designed for people with very large hands. However, most people don't have hands large enough to make full use of this instrument–much like not having super vision in small print world. Very few pianists have considered alternatives, due to the lack of awareness, lack of availability, and concern for being stigmatized for not using a conventional piano keyboard. In addition, many people actively oppose making an alternative form of piano acceptable for performance or competition.

It's hard to comprehend how this situation has persisted. There are many other activities in which a tool, instrument, or piece of equipment comes in various sizes to accommodate everyone's needs. Here are just two examples:

- Imagine trying to run a race in which all of the competitors are required to wear the same size shoes. Your feet are smaller than average, so you're constantly stumbling as you run, sometimes one of the shoes goes flying off your foot, and you must work hard to keep up with runners whose shoes fit perfectly.

- If you try to ride a bicycle built for someone much taller than you, your feet barely reach the pedals, you have to stretch your arms to grip the handlebars, and you can barely keep your balance, let alone get rolling.

In each of these cases, it's obvious that the problem is not you, it's the piece of equipment. We have custom sizes for everything under the sun–clothing, sports equipment, and even other musical instruments like violins and guitars. Why do we have only one size of piano keyboard?

This deficiency makes me feel like Jack from *Jack and the Beanstalk* when I play a conventional piano keyboard. For me and my smaller-than-average-male hands, the keyboard looks and feels like it was made for a giant. As we'll soon see, this is not far from the truth. Using a piano keyboard that doesn't fit one's hand size causes frustration, pain, and sometimes even injury–and it limits what a person with small hands is able to achieve on this instrument. Given the wide variation in hand size with race, gender, and age, it's hard to understand why everyone is expected to use the same size keyboard. Yet this is precisely the view that has become entrenched in piano manufacturing and in the world of performance and competition. Anyone struggling due to their smaller hand size is told to work harder, practice more, or choose a more suitable repertoire.

Common sense leads to a simple solution: narrower piano keyboards. Common sense is starting to fill a void in the musical world that has been present for more than a century, as there are now many options for narrower keyboards available. I am an advocate for DS6.0®[1], DS5.5®, and DS5.1 keyboards as alternatives to the conventional DS6.5 keyboard. In this book we will explore this simple, profoundly effective innovation through my own journey to acquire a properly sized keyboard.

---

[1] DS stands for Donison-Steinbuhler, the two men who pioneered the development and wider distribution of alternative sized piano keyboards. David Steinbuhler established several standards named according to the width of an octave (see Chapter 1 for an explanation of musical terms used in this book) on that keyboard. The conventional keyboard, having 6.5 inches per octave is designated the DS6.5 standard. The other most common standards are DS6.0, DS5.5, and DS5.1. These men and their keyboard standards are discussed in Chapter 5.

II III

Chapter 1

PIANO DIAGRAMS

Understanding the Piano Keyboard

Before we begin exploring the challenges introduced by the size of the conventional piano keyboard, it's important to understand its basic layout. Figure 1.1 shows a diagram of a keyboard with note names indicated. I'll briefly discuss the important points for you to understand. Don't worry–you will not need to know anything about the note names after this.

The piano keyboard comprises a repeating pattern of 12 keys. If you start from the left with the first white key that is marked C and move to the right, notice that there is a set of alternating white and black keys containing two black keys followed by a second set of alternating white and black keys containing three black keys. There is no black key between the two sets (between the keys labeled E and F), and the pattern then repeats with no black key between the repetition of the pattern (between the keys labeled B and C). You don't need to worry about these note names any more, and I'm rarely going to refer to them in the text. This discussion is just to help you understand the keyboard design and layout.

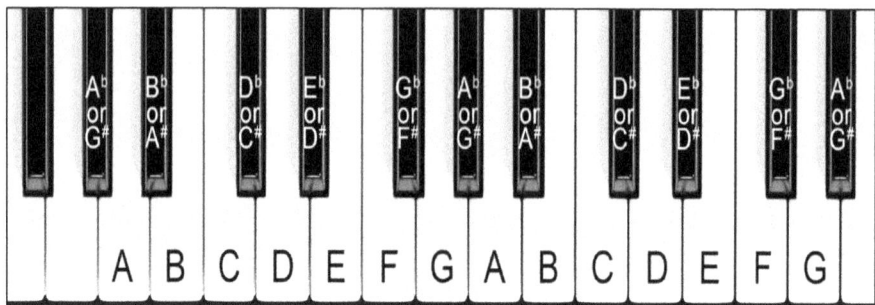

Figure 1.1 - Piano keyboard showing note names.

Each key that has the same note name indicated is the same pitch regardless of where on the keyboard it occurs. The only difference is how high or low it sounds. Moving from left to right, each set of 12 keys represents one octave–for example, the two white keys labeled C in the diagram above–and then the next octave begins, containing the exact same pitches but one level higher in sound.

The distance between two keys on the keyboard is called an interval. Intervals are formed when two keys are played in sequence, or when playing them at the same time. The shortest possible interval is a half step. There is a half step between any two adjacent keys on the piano. See Figures 1.2-1.4. Note that even though the white keys all look like they are adjacent to each other, in most cases there is a black key between two white keys. For example, in Figure 1.1, the first two white keys labeled C and D have a black key between them, labeled D^b or $C^#$.

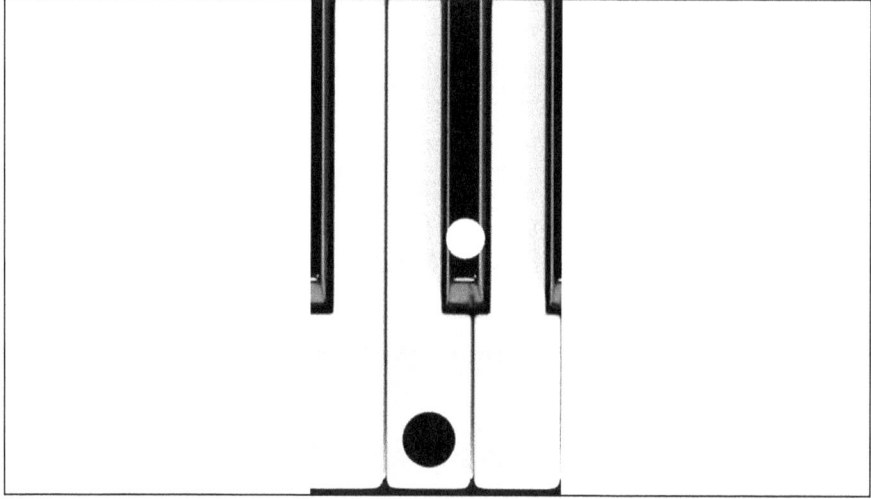

Figure 1.2 - Example of a half step from white key to black key.

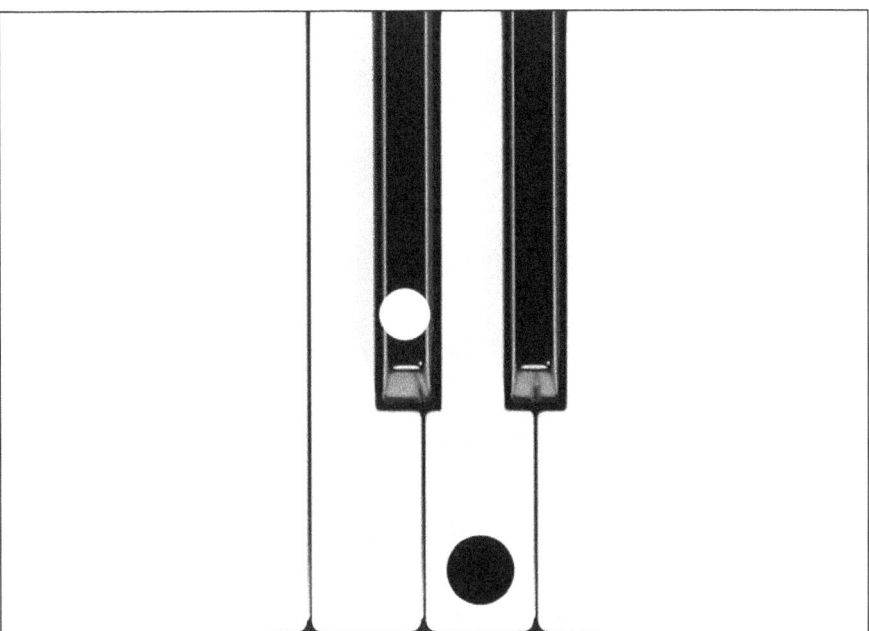

Figure 1.3 - Example of a half step from black key to white key.

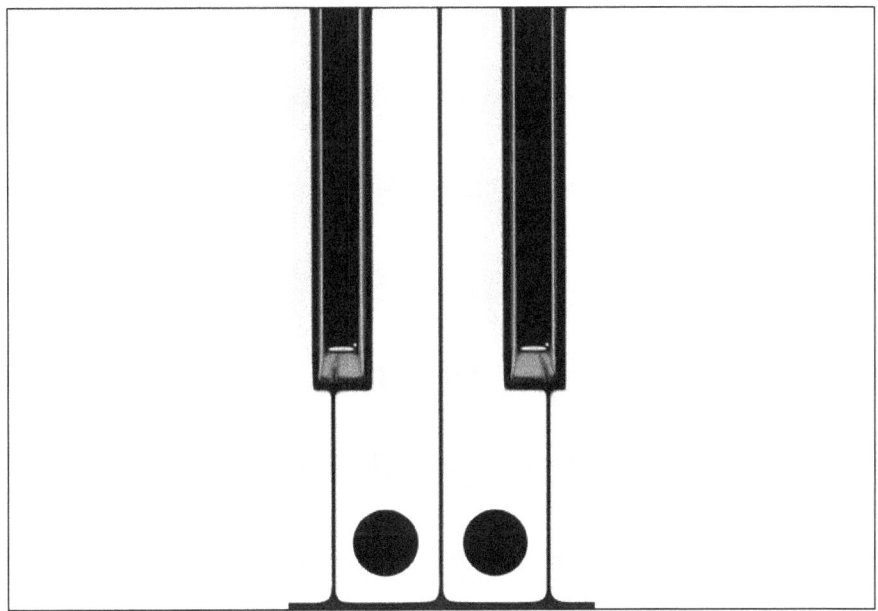

Figure 1.4 - Example of a half step from white key to white key.

A whole step occurs when you move from one key to another, skipping exactly one key in between. There are four ways this can happen on the piano keyboard as shown in Figures 1.5-1.8. There is always one key, whether it be black or white, between the two keys that make up the whole step. Again, remember that even though the white keys all look adjacent to each other, there is usually a black key between two white keys.

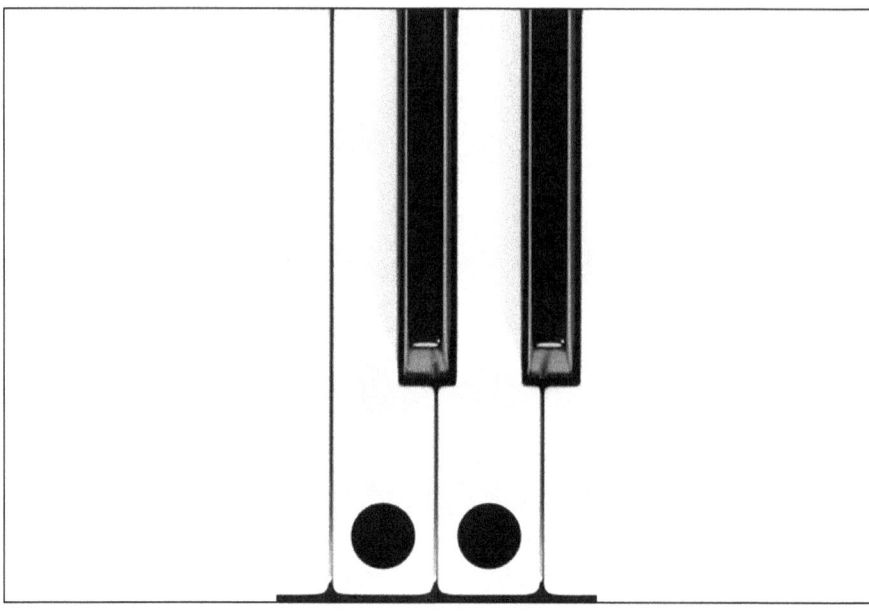

Figure 1.5 - Example of a whole step from white key to white key.

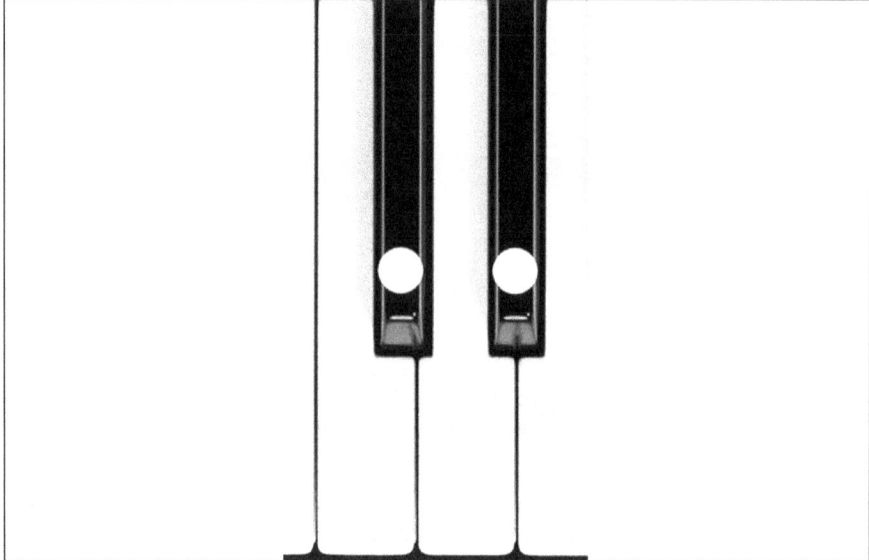

Figure 1.6 - Example of a whole step from black key to black key.

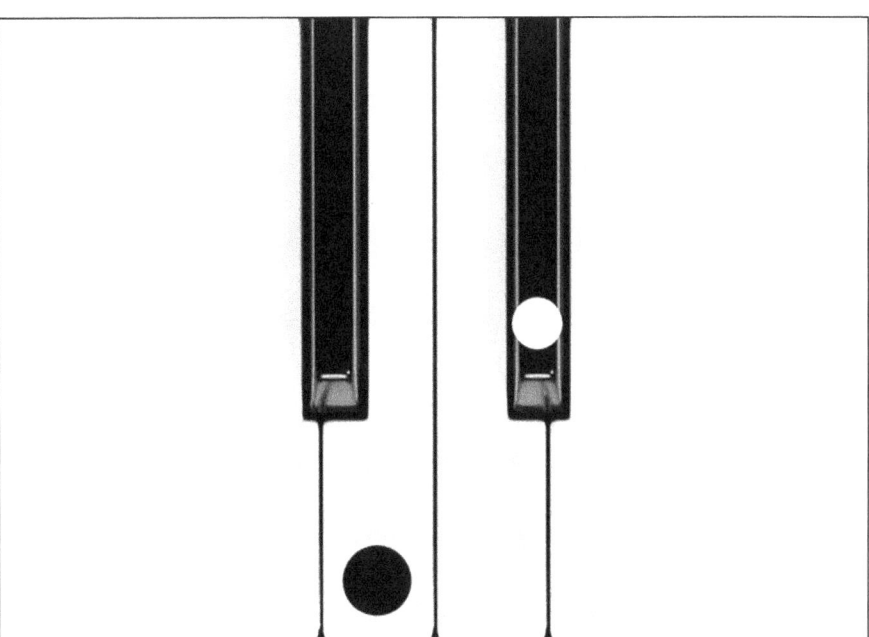

Figure 1.7 - Example of a whole step from white key to black key.

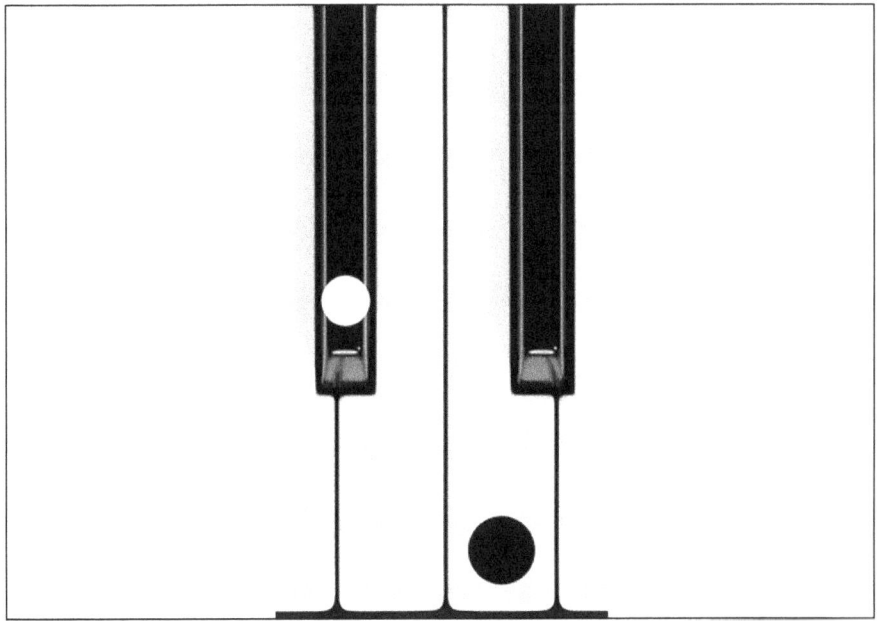

Figure 1.8 - Example of a whole step from black key to white key.

To illustrate concepts related to hand span and the physical demands of playing various chords on the piano, I will sometimes use musical notation to specify what I'm discussing; however, you do not need to be a piano player or other musician to understand the ideas in this book. For readers who do not read music and/or may not be familiar with the piano, each example will be accompanied by a diagram of a section of the piano keyboard showing which keys are notated in the music. Even experienced pianists may find these diagrams useful, as they visually represent the distances between keys and clearly show the physical reach required to play each chord, and that's all that really matters in this book. Here is an example:

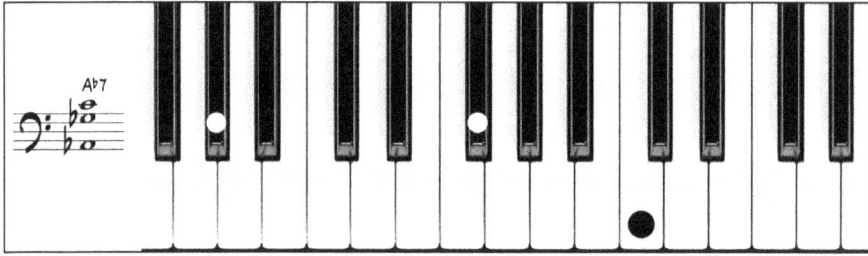

Figure 1.9 - Piano diagram example.

The dots on the keyboard indicate the keys corresponding to the musical chord notated on the left. Some examples will have multiple chords in the musical fragment. Each chord will be numbered, and the corresponding numbered piano diagram will appear below. Sometimes we won't need the musical notation, and only the piano diagram will be shown.

Throughout this book, I will be referring to intervals such as octaves, ninths, and tenths. It will be helpful to understand what these intervals mean and how they translate to the piano keyboard, so we will take a look at each of the larger intervals, beginning with an octave on the piano keyboard using the piano diagram format.

Remember, the piano keyboard is just a repeating pattern of 12 keys. When the pattern repeats, you have reached the next octave. So here's what an octave looks like on our piano diagram. Let's look at two examples, one on the white keys and the other on the black keys. Here is what an octave looks like between white keys:

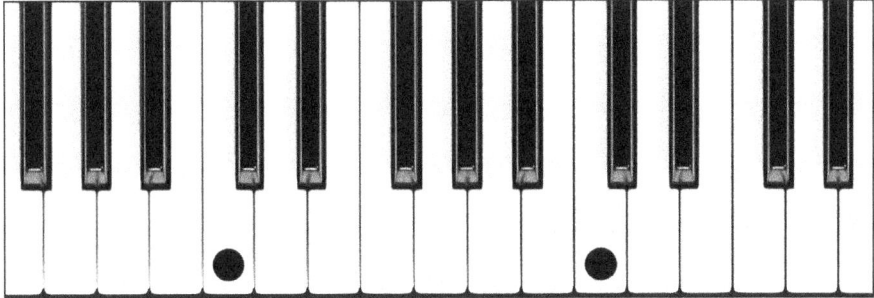

Figure 1.10 - Example of an octave between white keys.

To provide some perspective in these piano diagrams, here's a photograph of what my hand looks like playing the octave shown above between white keys on a conventional keyboard:

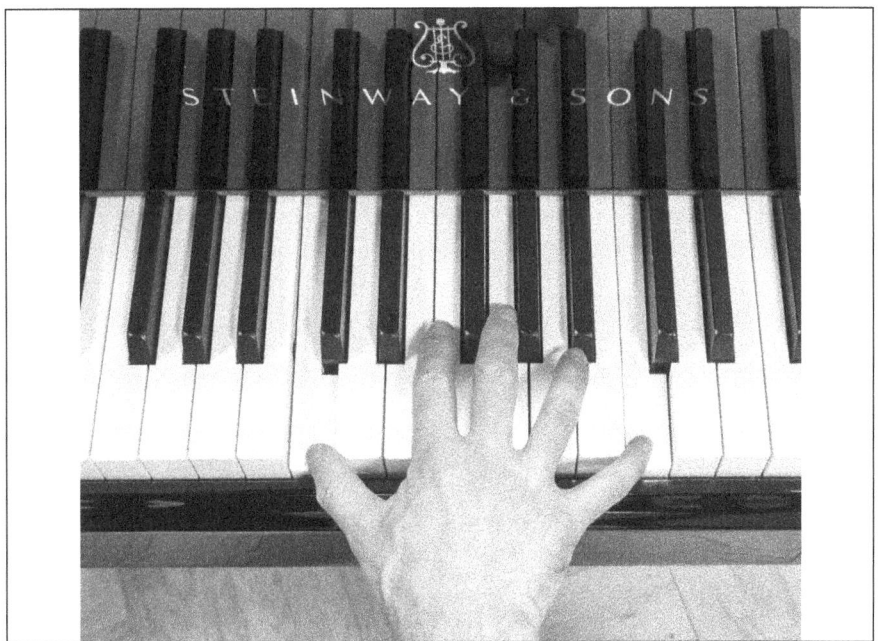

Figure 1.11 - My hand playing an octave between white keys on the conventional keyboard.

The next figure illustrates an octave between black keys.

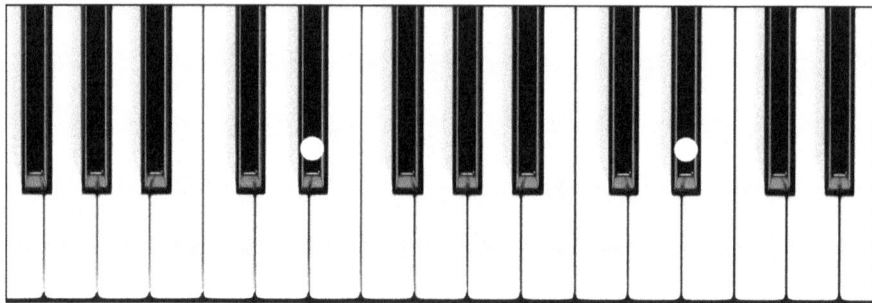

Figure 1.12 - Example of an octave between black keys.

As we move to the next largest interval (from octave to ninth, from ninth to tenth), we'll increase the interval size by a half step (to form what's called the minor ninth and minor tenth) and also by a whole step (to form what's called the major ninth and major tenth).

Now let's look at the next largest interval from an octave, a ninth. A ninth is one step (half or whole) larger than an octave. The next two figures illustrate examples of a minor ninth and a major ninth.

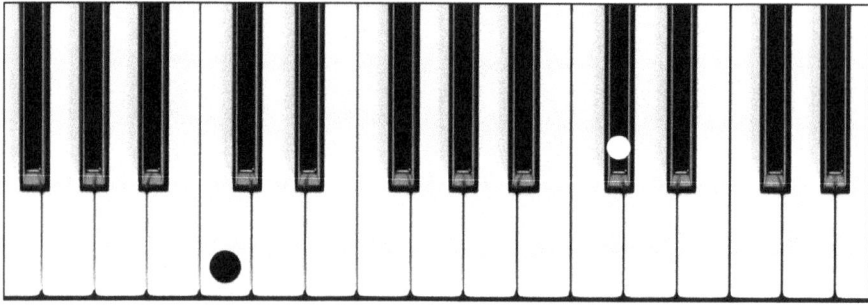

Figure 1.13 - Example of a minor ninth interval.

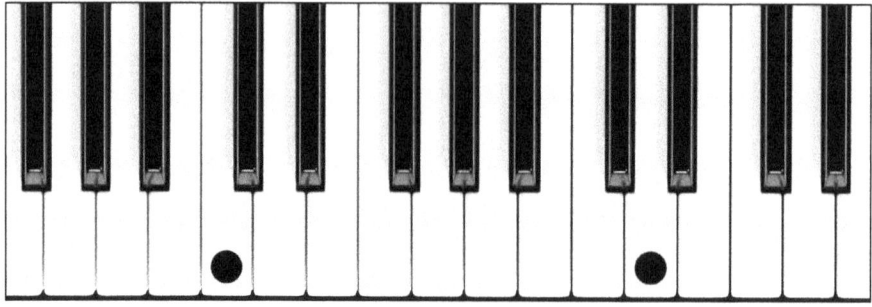

Figure 1.14 - Example of a major ninth interval.

Note that major intervals are always a little wider in distance between keys than minor intervals of the same name because there is an additional half step between the keys as can be seen in these examples of the two types of ninths.

If we increase the distance of the major ninth by an additional half or whole step, we reach the minor and major tenths, respectively. The next figures illustrate a minor tenth and a major tenth.

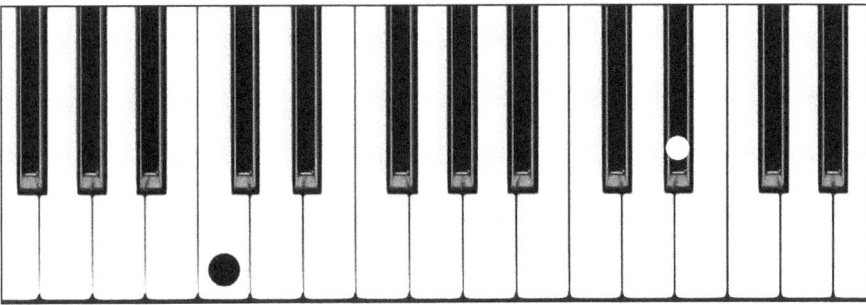

Figure 1.15 - Example of a minor tenth interval.

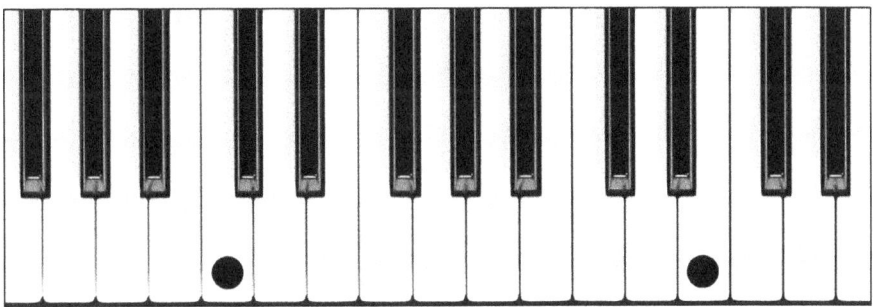

Figure 1.16 - Example of a major tenth interval.

You might assume that not all tenths span the same physical distance, depending on whether they begin and end on black or white keys–and you'd be absolutely right. This variation applies to all intervals, but for now, we'll examine a few additional examples of tenths to illustrate the point.

Among the shortest tenths are minor tenths between two black keys, as in Figure 1.17.

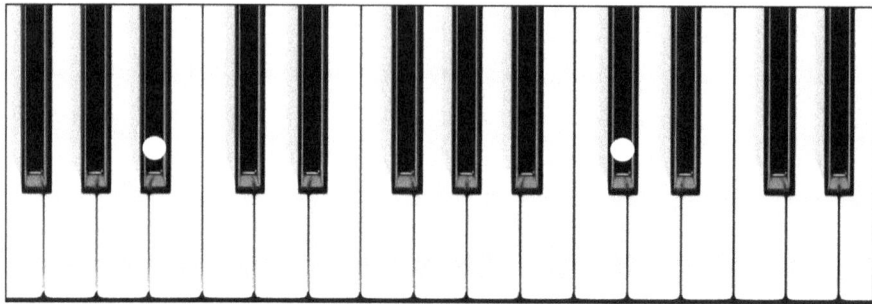

Figure 1.17 - Minor tenth between two black keys.

When major tenths start on a white key and end on a black key, or vice versa, they span a greater distance. The figures below show examples of some of the wider tenth intervals on the piano keyboard.

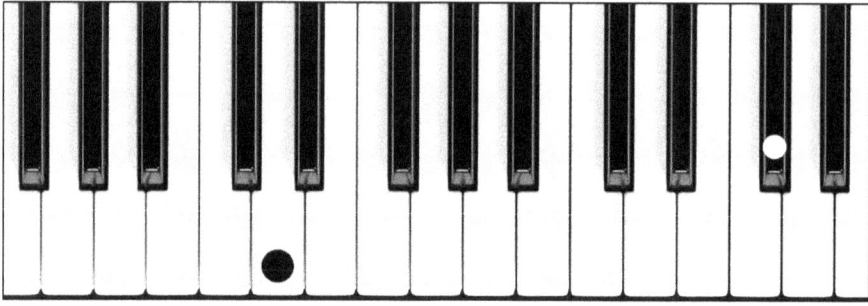

Figure 1.18 - Wider major tenth interval from white key to black key.

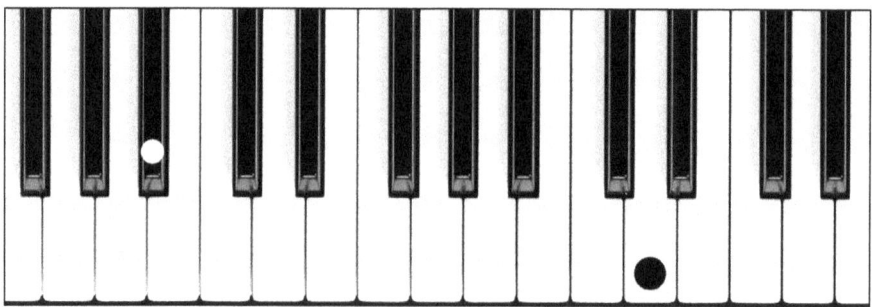

Figure 1.19 - Wider major tenth interval from black key to white key.

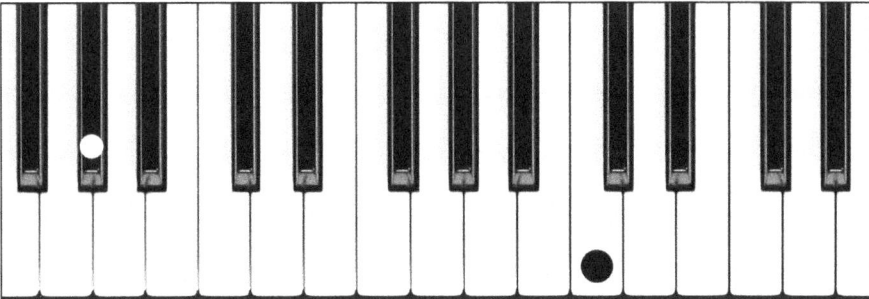

Figure 1.20 - Very wide major tenth interval from black key to white key.

Octaves, ninths, and tenths are the wider intervals we'll be most interested in. Likewise, intervals of other sizes are referred to by the number of steps they span. Here are examples of some shorter intervals I will sometimes mention:

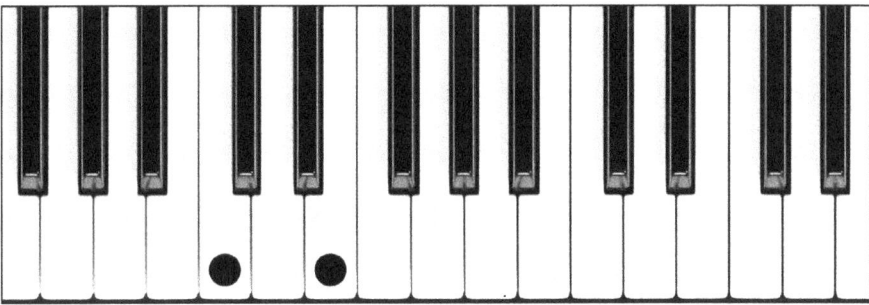

Figure 1.21 - Example of a major third interval.

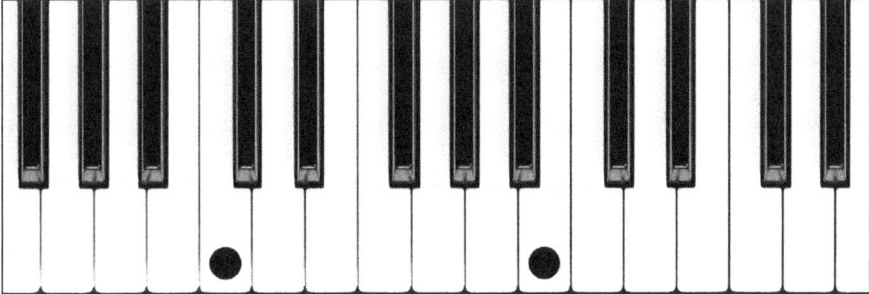

Figure 1.22 - Example of a major seventh interval.

Now that you have a clearer understanding of the piano keyboard and the physical layout of some of the wider intervals often used in playing many kinds of music, we can begin to examine how the conventional keyboard size influences a pianist's capacity to fully utilize the instrument. In the next chapter, we will explore the history of the piano keyboard and the norms surrounding it, uncovering how its current dimensions were established and what has resulted from the widespread acceptance of those dimensions.

Chapter 2

KEYS TO TRADITION

The Evolution, Challenges, and Enduring Norms of the Piano Keyboard

The size and dimensions of the piano keyboard have been universally accepted by both piano manufacturers and pianists for nearly 150 years. This widespread acceptance has led to the idea that the piano keyboard is standardized to its current dimensions. Throughout this book, however, I am careful to always refer to the traditional piano keyboard as "conventional" or sometimes "traditional," consciously choosing not to refer to it as "standard" because conventional and traditional are more accurate terms.

There is in fact no standard piano key width and keyboard dimension. As we'll soon see, the size of 6.5 inches per octave was settled on as a convention adopted universally by piano manufacturers in the 1880s for practical reasons. There are no standards agencies that set the rules for piano keyboards. It is a simple convention, and in fact there are minor variations among keyboards from different manufacturers.

For example, I once encountered a Baldwin having a conventional keyboard on which I could barely play a tenth interval from black key to black key, normally an impossible feat for me on a conventional keyboard. I also once owned a 61-key Yamaha digital keyboard with supposedly conventional size keys on which I could just reach a minor tenth from white to black key in addition to the shorter black to black tenths. These small variations are most likely due primarily to manufacturing tolerances, but they can sometimes be noticeable as in these cases.

Nevertheless, when a pianist sits down at a piano, he expects the keyboard to be exactly the same size as on every other piano he plays. How did we arrive at this convention?

A Brief History of the Piano Keyboard

People today are so accustomed to a single piano keyboard size that they would probably be surprised to learn that keyboard sizes have varied widely since at least the mid-16th century. From the late 18th century through the mid-19th century, most keyboards actually featured narrower keys than what we find in today's pianos. Much of the classic piano repertoire, composed between 1750 and 1850, was written for these smaller keyboards, and pieces from this era rarely required intervals greater than an octave.[2]

During the 1800s, the development and popularization of the piano was also shaped by influential European composers and virtuosos such as Liszt and Kalkbrenner, who collaborated closely with major piano manufacturers and were central figures in public performances and marketing campaigns. Renowned pianists like Anton Rubinstein and Paderewski helped promote Steinway pianos through extensive tours in the United States in the late nineteenth century.[3]

---

[2] "Keyboard History." *Pianists for Alternatively Sized Keyboards,* https://paskpiano.org/keyboard-history/. Accessed July 13, 2025.
[3] Ibid.

Around 1880, piano manufacturers, influenced by the needs of these prominent European male virtuoso pianists, began designing instruments with wider keys. This change was driven by the desire to produce a bigger sound suitable for large concert halls, which required innovations like cross-stringing and larger soundboards.[4]

Ideally, each piano key would always align precisely with the hammer and strings it is connected to. As the soundboard was made larger to produce a bigger sound, however, the overall size of the piano increased, and the hammers and strings were spread out more widely to take advantage of the larger soundboard. It became increasingly necessary to widen the keys so that they stayed aligned with the hammers and strings as much as possible.

If the keys were not widened, each key would be offset from the hammer and strings it was ultimately connected to, and the resulting angle, or key flare, would both simultaneously decrease the power that could be delivered through the keys and increase the structural stresses on the keys.[5] The slightly wider keys helped minimize the angle of key flare on these larger instruments and helped keep the keys aligned with their hammers and strings. The wider keys caused no problems for the large-handed male performers who dominated the concert stage at the time.[6]

The octave span that resulted from these design changes was 6.5 inches. As we'll see, this size keyboard is optimally tailored to pianists who have very large hands like the male European virtuosos from the end of the 19th century. Those who have smaller hands are at a distinct disadvantage in playing the conventional piano keyboard.

The 6.5-inch octave keyboard became the convention for virtually all acoustic piano manufacturers, for both grand pianos and uprights. Digital piano and keyboard makers later adopted the same dimensions to match the acoustic instruments.

---

[4] Ibid.

[5] The narrower keyboards we will discuss in later chapters have a high degree of key flare– especially at the extreme ends of the keyboard–since the keys are offset from their hammers and strings. This is exactly the problem the manufacturers in the 1880s were trying to avoid. The loss of power and increased structural stresses must be addressed in acoustic narrower keyboards, and we'll see how that was accomplished in Chapter 5.

[6] *Pianists for Alternatively Sized Keyboards,* "Keyboard History."

An Enduring Norm and Its Consequences

The convention of a 6.5-inch octave has persisted for nearly 150 years. When people look at the piano's familiar pattern of white and black keys, the idea of there being more than one piano size never crosses their mind. Children and adults of all ages learn to play "the piano", performers play "the piano", "the piano" appears in movies and commercials, and the expectation is that it's the exact same size in every situation. It never even occurs to most people that it doesn't "fit" all pianists, any more than a single racket would fit all tennis players.

The widespread acceptance and reluctance to question the traditional keyboard also stems from the fact that, until recently, it has been the only option available. Since most have managed to cope with it up to now, the question arises: is there really a need to change it?

Indeed, when faced with the challenges of having smaller hands and approaching repertoire that requires a larger hand span, pianists often internalize any difficulties as personal limitations rather than inherent challenges presented by the instrument itself. Piano students almost always focus on technique, exercises, hand stretches, fingering changes, additional practice, dropping notes, or even complete avoidance of some repertoire. They often think to themselves, "I wish I had bigger hands." The thought of "I wish the piano keyboard weren't so wide" never even occurs to them.

More than thirty years ago, a few free-thinking people began to question these assumptions and envision how having a piano with narrower keys would completely eliminate all of these problems. My personal experience as a jazz pianist is a case in point for the value of these custom keyboards. In the chapters that follow, I'll describe the practical challenges I've faced and musical opportunities I've missed.

I am a jazz pianist, and to understand the style of jazz piano I prefer, we will now turn to Oscar Peterson, the great Canadian jazz pianist. Oscar Peterson was not only a musical giant–his remarkably large hands were a perfect match for the conventional keyboard.

Chapter 3

OSCAR PETERSON

A Musical Giant

Oscar Peterson (1925-2007) was a Canadian jazz pianist and is widely regarded as among the best jazz pianists of all time. Some consider him the best, some consider him second only to Art Tatum, but everyone recognizes his virtuosity and keen ability to swing. I consider him one of the best pianists in any genre. He was a technical master, capable of the greatest of pianistic feats.

Music has been part of my life from an early age, but I didn't discover Oscar Peterson until 10th grade in high school. At the age of 7, I started piano lessons, beginning with the basics of music and the keyboard, and eventually focusing on classical music. A few years later I took up the saxophone and played in jazz bands every year from the 5th grade all the way through my time in college and graduate school. I was even a semi-professional musician in college and graduate school, playing alto and baritone saxophone in a 20-piece big band that performed at weddings and other paid gigs.

Figure 3.1 - Oscar Peterson in Seattle, 2004.[7]

My first time hearing Oscar's music was unforgettable. I was 16 years old relaxing in my bedroom in the evening, listening to the local Pittsburgh radio show, *The Nightside with Tony Mowod.* The tune he was broadcasting was "Kelly's Blues", written by Oscar for his wife, a recording made in 1990 at the Blue Note in New York City. Oscar played with a quartet featuring Ray Brown on bass, Herb Ellis on guitar, and Bobby Durham on drums. Oscar's playing instantly enthralled me, and I found myself completely absorbed in

---

[7] Photograph by the author. Published with permission of the estate of Oscar Peterson.

the 12-minute recording. Every chorus he played introduced new, interesting musical ideas that seemed to build with energy as the tune progressed. His virtuosity was unmistakable. He played many, many notes, each and every one with its purpose. It was so melodic and harmonically rich. And his rhythm–it swung like nobody's business!

Oscar's comping during Herb Ellis's guitar solo was impeccably rhythmic and precisely timed, delivering exactly what the solo needed to shine and driving Herb Ellis's performance to reach new creative heights. His playing of a walking bass line in the left hand during Ray Brown's bass solo remains the gold standard for me whenever I approach blues bass lines. The entire performance was mesmerizing–it embodied everything I envisioned jazz piano to be.

The very next thing I did was buy the CD, *Saturday Night at the Blue Note,* and at this point I cannot count the number of times I've listened to that album. It became the foundation of my now extensive Oscar Peterson collection.

My greatest wish as a jazz lover was to see Oscar Peterson perform live. After suffering a stroke in 1993 that severely impacted his ability to use his left hand, however, his public appearances became increasingly rare. By the early 2000s, catching him in concert was like finding a rare jewel; and with the internet still in its infancy, learning where he'd be playing next was no easy task. More than once, after a newly released live CD hit the shelves, I realized with regret that I had missed yet another chance to see him in person.

Around 2000, I met professional jazz pianist Jim Martinez, renowned for his tribute concerts to Oscar. In conversation, he casually mentioned attending one of the very concerts that would later be immortalized on CD–a recording I treasured. Naturally, I had to know his secret. He connected me with Oscar's secretary, who, to my eternal gratitude, graciously tolerated my occasional inquiries about upcoming performances.

Then in 2002 the message I'd been waiting for finally arrived: Oscar Peterson would be performing in Philadelphia at the Kimmel Center for the Performing Arts. I received the exciting news on a

Friday in September, and the performance was scheduled for that Sunday, two days later. I was able to buy tickets at the last minute, and I made the trip without a moment's hesitation. The anticipation was overwhelming; the night itself, a memory I will treasure forever. Every note was everything I'd hoped for and more.

That first concert opened the door to a remarkable chapter in my life. Over the next few years up until Oscar's passing in 2007, I planned my vacations around his performances, traveling to his concerts in New York, Seattle, San Francisco, Montreal, London, and Manchester. Each performance was its own magic, and together they formed some of the brightest memories of my musical journey. On several occasions I even had the honor and joy of meeting Oscar and spending a few, brief moments with him. Looking back now, I feel deeply fortunate and profoundly grateful to have witnessed the genius of Oscar Peterson in person, time and time again.

Oscar's music has profoundly shaped my musical identity. Whenever I hear music in my mind–whether mentally replaying something I've heard before or imagining my own improvisational ideas–it feels as though he's right there beside me, feeding me the vocabulary, rhythm, and soul that defined his artistry. His imprint on my music is palpable, and this connection is nearly constant. It's the soundtrack of my life, weaving through my thoughts and emotions like a faithful companion.

This is how important Oscar Peterson's music is to me. This is the deep level of enjoyment I have experienced listening to him. So it follows that as I started to shift into playing jazz piano–which I did once I finished graduate school and had difficulty finding an outlet for playing the saxophone–the style I wanted to emulate was Oscar Peterson's.

My jazz knowledge and skills were limited to saxophone, so I needed to start to learn more formally how to play jazz piano. As I began my studies, it was not long before I ran headlong into my greatest obstacle in playing solo jazz piano, especially in the style of Oscar Peterson: my physical inability to reach a tenth interval.

Chapter 4

JAZZ PIANO

Exploring the Limitations of Smaller Hands

In the discussion to follow, I approach the topic of why options for narrower piano keyboards are needed from my personal experience as a jazz pianist, focusing solely on the practical challenges and missed musical opportunities I have encountered in my own playing. My perspective is shaped by the demands of jazz repertoire–such as wide voicings, complex chords, and rapid leaps–that often require stretches beyond what feels comfortable or even possible on a conventional keyboard. I am not drawing on research, surveys, or the experiences of pianists in other genres, nor am I referencing data about hand sizes in the broader population in this chapter. (We will explore empirical data on hand spans in Chapter 6.) My observations here are rooted in the day-to-day realities of performing and practicing jazz, and the ways in which the conventional keyboard excludes me and others from some musical possibilities and imposes physical pain and strain on us during everyday play.

Solo Jazz Piano

The difficulties I have faced playing the conventional piano keyboard are most evident when playing solo jazz piano. The solo pianist must fill several roles simultaneously. He must play the bass, establish the harmonic structure and flow, and play the melody. Plus, all of this has to be done while creating a rhythmic flow to the music. Let's take a look at some of the requirements of solo jazz piano that are impacted by hand size.

Shared-Hand Voicings

A voicing is the selection of notes that make up a chord and how the pianist chooses to arrange them on the keyboard. In *Playing Solo Jazz Piano,* Jeremy Siskind describes one of the key concepts often used in solo jazz piano, shared-hand voicings:

> *Many styles of solo piano involve a[n] ... even division of labor in which the right hand plays the melody, the left hand plays the bass, and the two hands share the midrange chords. Although it oversimplifies the concept, it is useful to think about the third, fourth, and fifth fingers of the right hand as dedicated to the melody, the third, fourth, and fifth fingers of the left hand as dedicated to the bass, and the thumbs and index fingers of both hands as dedicated to the chords.*[8]

Figure 4.1 visually illustrates this hand configuration. As Siskind points out, this is a simplification, and the roles of the parts of the hand may change on the fly. But if all three parts are required at once, then this is the typical hand configuration, and it requires the two hands to cover a broad stretch of real estate on the keyboard. With smaller hands (i.e., hands that cannot reach a tenth), this almost always means leaving something out either by dropping the bass or excluding part of the harmony. Or it means choosing chord voicings that fit within the player's hand span and excluding other, often more

---

[8] Siskind, Jeremy. *Playing Solo Jazz Piano,* edited by Gail Lew, Jeremy Siskind Music Publishing, 2020, p. 66.

desirable voicing options. Alternatively, the player can roll the chords by playing each note separately, with a very fast leap from the root to the tenth. In this way, all the voices sound, just not together at the same time initially. Some combination of these options can work depending on the execution, but it is very limiting for the player.

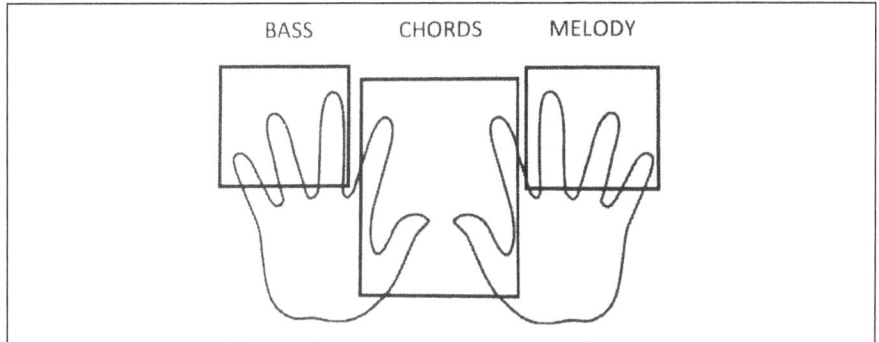

Figure 4.1 - Illustration of hand position for shared-hand voicings.[9]

With smaller hands, it is physically impossible for me to play some of the larger chords that enrich the sound of the music and help give it some of the signature Oscar Peterson style. This was a challenge I faced immediately, and it was frustrating knowing what I wanted to play but being incapable of playing it. No matter how much I practiced or stretched, I would never be able to reach those chords.

Chord Voicing Examples

Let's look at some specific examples of voicings I often want to use when playing jazz piano. We'll focus mainly on the left hand, which typically plays wider chords much more frequently than the right hand.

It's worth noting, however, that with the shared-hand voicings described above, the top note played by the thumb of the left hand can sometimes be played by the thumb of the right hand instead. Unfortunately, this rarely solves the problem of having to reach a tenth. The challenge is simply transferred to the right hand. The total distance between the lowest and highest notes in the chord and the

---

[9] Ibid. Diagram reproduced with permission of the author.

inclusion of intermediary notes that fill in the harmony between these extremes very frequently leads to one hand or the other having to stretch a tenth to reach all the desired notes.

Let's start by examining some common voicings used in the left hand to play one type of chord, a C7 chord. The chord name doesn't matter–we're just going to look at different commonly-used voicings to see how much distance they span on the keyboard. I will be referring to the various notes of the chord as the root, third, fifth, and seventh. The following figure displays a basic C7 chord. Starting from the left, the first marked key is the root, and the following keys are the third, fifth, and seventh of the chord, in order.

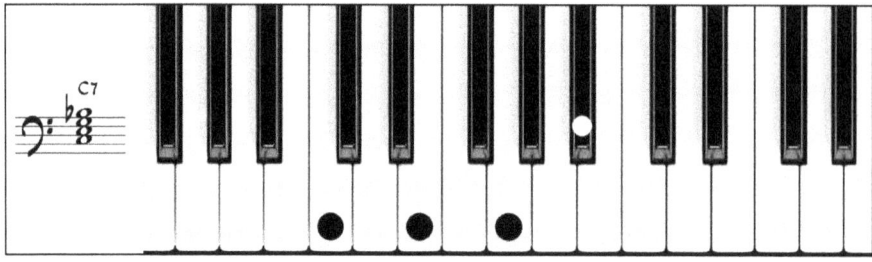

Figure 4.2 - Basic C7 chord voicing.

If the C7 chord we're discussing is voiced this way, all the keys fall within a single octave on the keyboard, so there is no problem reaching this entire chord unless you are a child or someone with extremely small hands. This is not the typical way to play the chord in most contexts, however. Instead, players usually voice the chord in the left hand using several different approaches. First, assume there is a bass player who will be playing the root of the chord, so the left hand does not need to play the root. The fifth of the chord adds color and texture to the sound, but it does not alter the essential character of the chord, so it can be dropped as well. This leaves us with the third and seventh of the chord. These notes form what is called a shell–the minimum harmonic information needed to identify what kind of chord it is. Shell voicings are very simple–just two notes–yet very commonly used. Here's what this shell voicing looks like for our C7 chord:

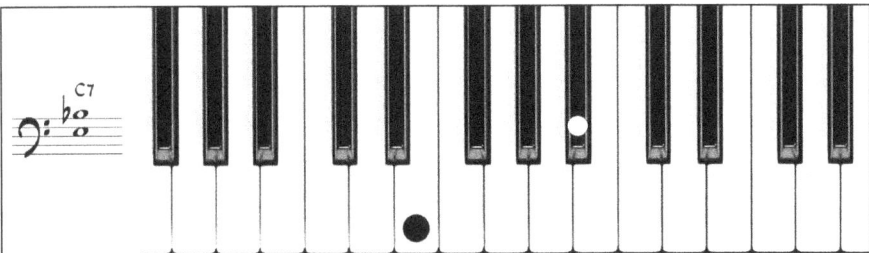

Figure 4.3 - C7 shell voicing without the root in the bass.

We can also reverse the order of these two notes and form a voicing with the seventh on bottom and the third on top:

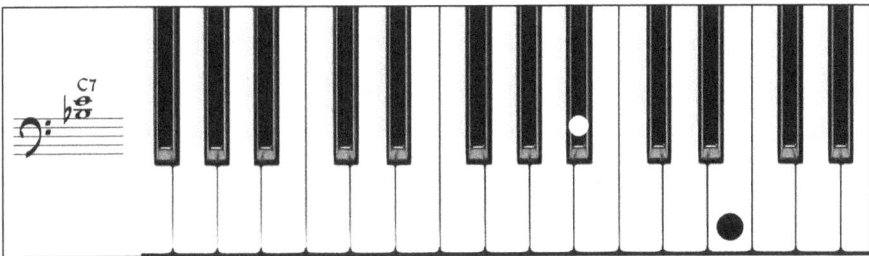

Figure 4.4 - Alternative C7 shell voicing without the root in the bass.

Here is another voicing of the same chord where we've added one additional note (the ninth) to add color to the sound:

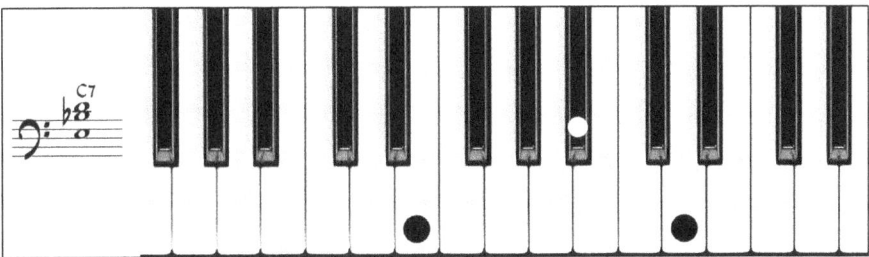

Figure 4.5 - C7 chord voicing with additional note (the ninth) added.

All these voicings fall within one octave, and this works perfectly well if there is a bass player. But when playing solo piano, the pianist needs to fulfill the role of the bass player as well. Figure 4.6 on the next page shows a basic voicing that includes the root in the bass.

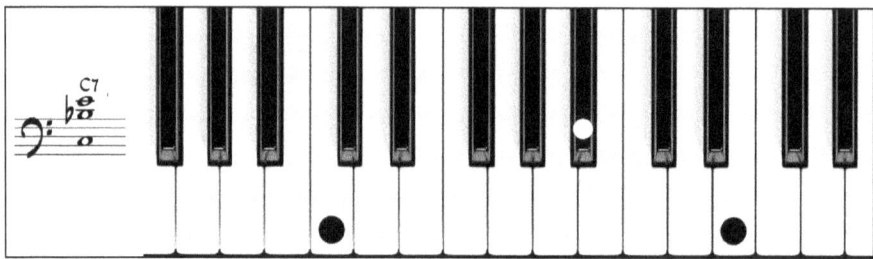

Figure 4.6 - C7 voicing including the root in the bass.

This voicing includes a tenth interval between the bottom and top notes, and it produces a full, rich sound because of the spread of the voicing. You could also play it as in Figure 4.7 with the top note lowered by an octave in order to eliminate the tenth interval, but this doesn't have the same rich sound as the voicing in Figure 4.6, and it creates new problems. You want the bottom note to be low on the keyboard–in the bass section–but if it is played too low, the whole chord sounds very muddy because of the proximity of two very low notes (the two white keys in Figure 4.7). The magnitude of this problem depends on which key signature you're playing in. You can resolve this issue by moving the chord an octave higher, but then it loses the power of the deep bass.

Also notice that this voicing is essentially the same as Figure 4.2, which I mentioned is not often used. One of the reasons for this, which affects the current voicing as well, is that these voicings have a much more closed, clustered sound since all the chord tones are contained within one octave. When there are more than two notes in the chord, it can start to have this clustered sound. In some contexts, that is a desirable sound, but when choosing a voicing that conveys both the bass and harmony, it is far less desirable. In contrast, the voicing in Figure 4.6 is spread over more than one octave, which gives that voicing a more open and breathable sound.

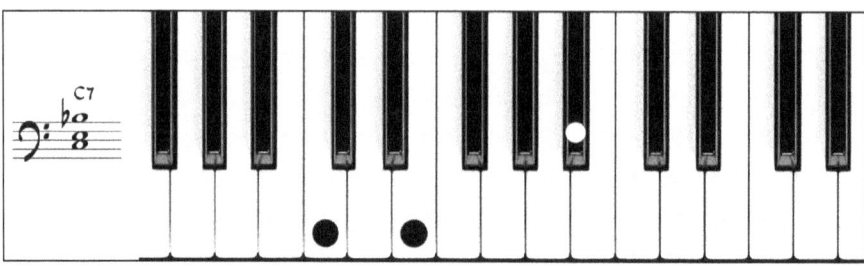

Figure 4.7 - Dropping the tenth down an octave.

You could also just play a seventh and leave out the third/tenth, like this:

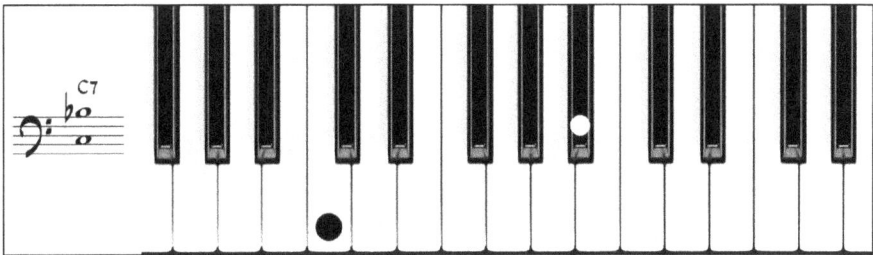

Figure 4.8 - C7 voicing excluding the third altogether.

This voicing is often used even by pianists who are able to reach tenths, however it is not ideal to use it exclusively. It leaves out the third of the chord, a critical tone in defining the sound of the chord. I used to have to play sevenths like this all the time, never able to get the richer tenth sound unless my right hand was able to jump down and add it as part of a two-handed voicing. This limitation made things difficult and frustrating for me.

In the wider version of the chord voicing, Figure 4.6, the bottom and top notes span a major tenth interval. In the key I've selected (C) the tenth interval is wide (it is, after all, a tenth), but it's not overly wide. Now take a look at this same voicing in a couple additional keys, using some of the larger tenths mentioned in Chapter 1:

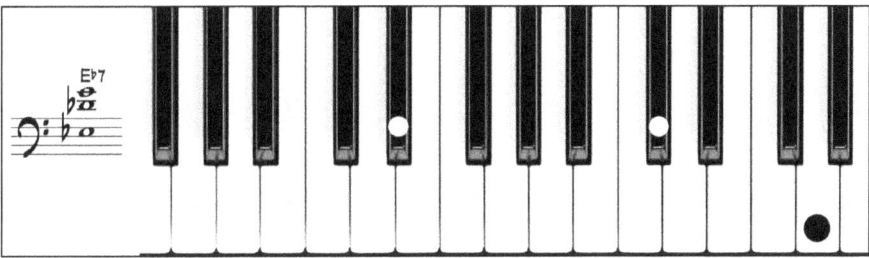

Figure 4.9 - E♭7 voicing containing a wider tenth interval.

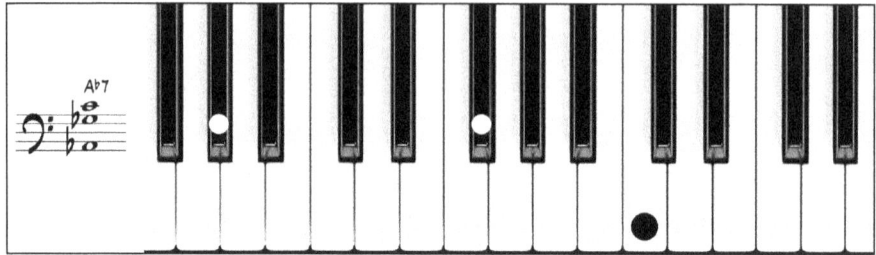

Figure 4.10 - A♭7 voicing containing a very wide tenth interval.

These chords are much more difficult to play, requiring a much wider hand span and stretch. Also keep in mind that we're not simply playing a tenth interval here. There is an intermediate note that has to be played, generally by the index finger, and that makes it even more important to have a larger hand span to be able to play these chords. Even pianists who are considered to have large hands (categorized as Zone C; see Chapter 6) have trouble with these voicings. Only people with very large hands (Zone D) are able to play them without issue.

Moving on to the right hand, one common phrase is known as the Count Basie ending. Figure 4.11 illustrates what it looks like. Again, the distance between the bottom and top notes of all three chords in this phrase is a tenth, in this case a minor tenth. The minor tenth makes the chord span a little smaller than it would be with a major tenth, but there are two other notes filling out each of the chords, and that makes this pattern very difficult to play–especially in every key–without very large hands.

Stride Piano

One style of jazz piano that presents physical challenges for people with smaller hands is stride, which Oscar Peterson features often in his solo playing. Basic stride piano is a style based on ragtime where the left hand alternates between a low bass note and a mid-range chord, usually a simple triad or seventh chord, or in more modern versions of stride, a typical left-hand voicing. The bass note is played on beats one and three, and the chord is played on beats two and four.[10]

---

[10] Ibid., 8-9.

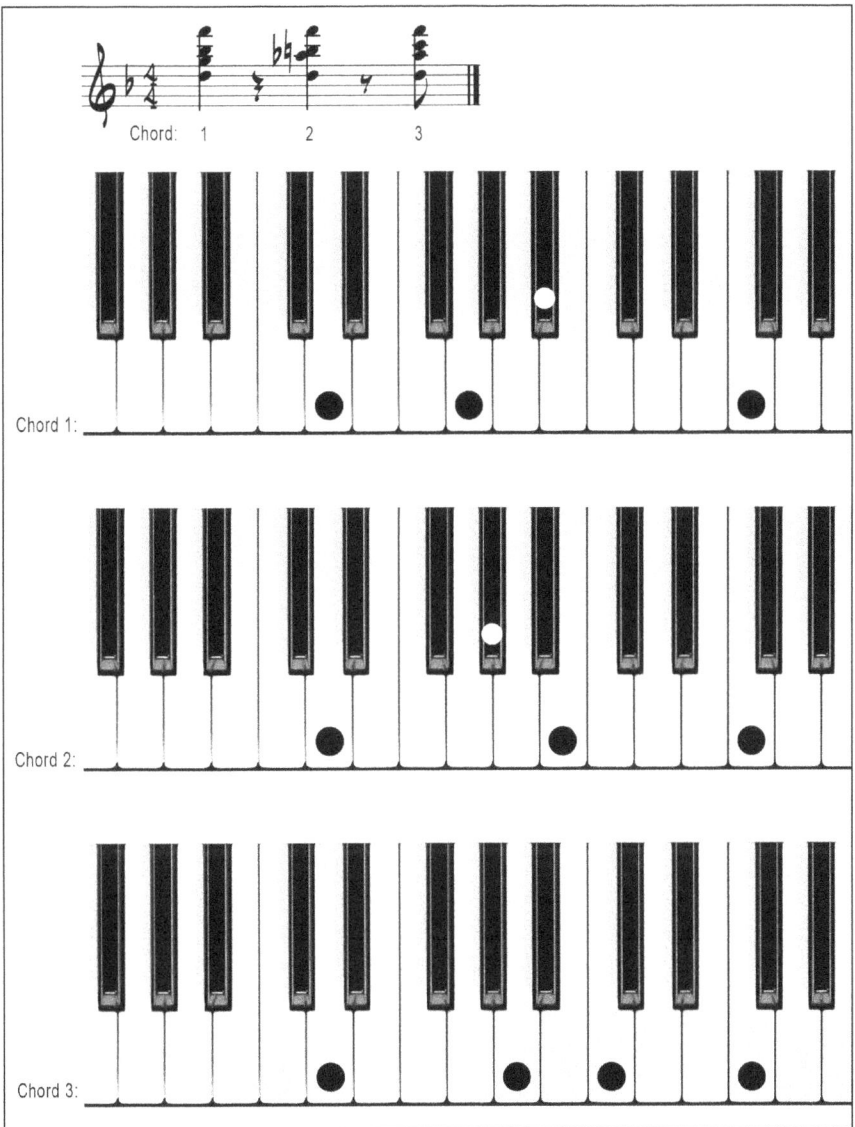

Figure 4.11 - The Count Basie ending.

This alternating pattern creates a characteristic "oompa" type of sound as the left hand strides between the low bass note and higher chord repeatedly. This simple stride pattern does not cause problems for smaller-handed individuals, at least in terms of the intervals involved. As described so far, there are no tenth intervals, just single notes, octaves, or fifths on the bottom, and a maximum spread of a seventh interval in the upper chord, so we won't take a look at any music or piano diagrams just yet.

What makes this pattern more difficult for smaller-handed players is that there is a significant jump between the bass note and the chord. On the conventional keyboard, this jump is large relative to the small-handed player's hand size, so it takes a more significant arm motion to make the leap, as well as some additional practice to ensure accuracy in landing on the chord and then leaping back down to the bass for the next cycle. Further, stride piano is often played at a very high speed, which compounds the difficulty of playing it. This isn't much of a problem for pianists with larger hands; but it is something that can be perfected with practice even by the smaller-handed pianist.

The basic ragtime-based stride pattern described above is rudimentary. More sophisticated styles of stride typically include seventh and/or tenth intervals rather than just the root, fifth, or octave for the bass part of the pattern. The reason for including sevenths and tenths is because of the harmonic richness those additional notes introduce. If the bottom note is the root, then the tenth above is equivalent to the third of the chord. The third and seventh are both critical harmonic components that together define the character of the chord. The tenth is especially useful because of the wide gap between it and the root. It helps create an open and full, rich sound. Figure 4.12 shows an example of a stride pattern using both sevenths and tenths.

Note that in this example, a small-handed pianist would not be able to play the tenth chord on the first beat. The only options would be to drop the tenth and play just the root, switch it to an octave or fifth, or roll the chord (playing each note separately, which requires a very fast leap from the root to the tenth). None of these options is optimal. This pattern would repeat with a tenth chord on beats one and/or three on most measures. As noted earlier, this pattern could potentially be played at very high tempo, compounding the difficulties for small-handed players.

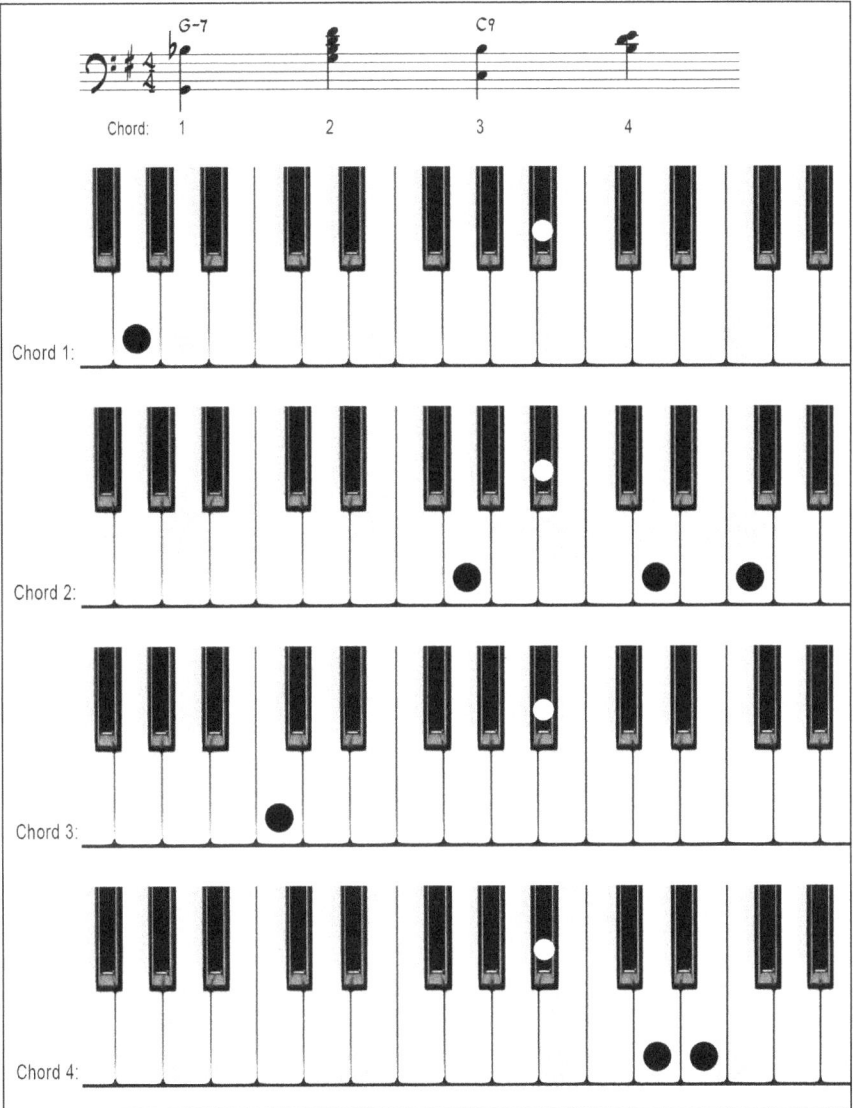

Figure 4.12 - Simple left-hand stride piano pattern.

Another common technique in stride piano is the use of walking tenths. This is a useful technique when changing from one chord to another, such as when switching from the root chord to the fourth chord in a stride blues as illustrated in Figure 4.13 in the key of E^b. Here, the left hand is "walking" down from E^b to A^{b11}. This is a highly effective technique because the bottom note is simply walking down the root of the chord, which clearly defines the harmonic basis of what's going on and in many cases is exactly what the bass player would play if there were one. Meanwhile, the top note is walking down on the thirds in parallel, which creates a richly harmonic sound. And again, because the two notes are so widely spread, there is a lot of clarity and openness in the sound.

This pattern could also be played at a very high tempo. At higher speeds, even people with larger hands who can reach these tenths will struggle to play this line quickly and accurately while maintaining fluidity. To achieve a smooth, legato feel, it helps tremendously to have very large hands that can flex from one chord to the next rather than having to stay fully stretched out the entire time. Ideally, if the player's hand is large enough to play a tenth between the thumb and fourth finger, they could alternate the bottom note between the pinky and fourth finger. This is the optimal way of playing this kind of pattern at a very high speed, and it is exactly how Oscar Peterson would play it, as evidenced by numerous video recordings.

Whenever a series of chords includes both the root and the tenth–whether as part of a walking tenth bass line or as chords played in a typical stride piano pattern–it creates the effect of two distinct musical lines happening simultaneously. These two lines move in parallel, almost as if a second hand were playing independently alongside the first. This dual-line texture gives stride piano its rich, layered sound and rhythmic complexity.

---

[11] I know we've been using some note names, but don't worry about them. As mentioned earlier, it doesn't really matter. Just take a look at the piano diagrams to understand how widely spaced these chords are.

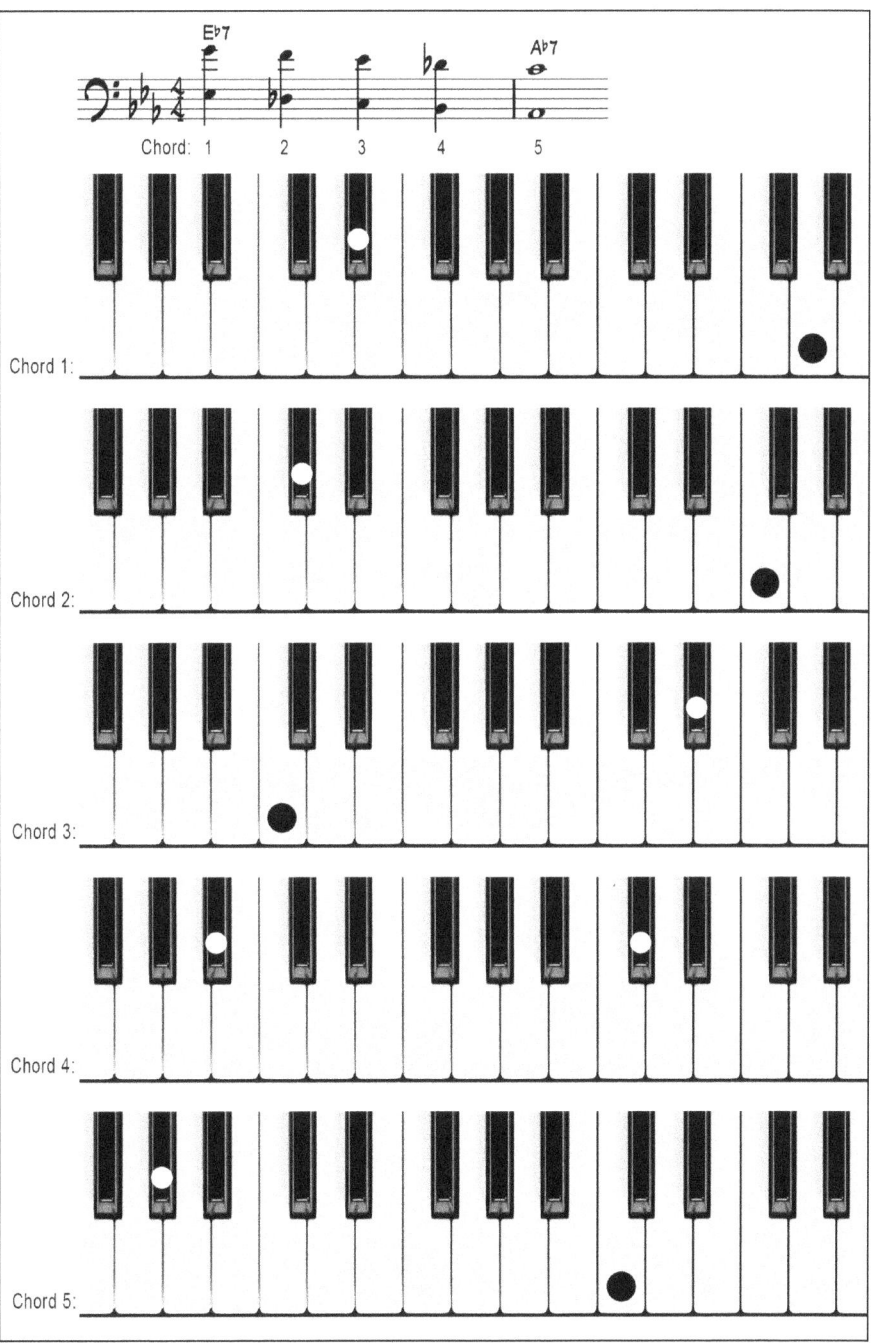

Figure 4.13 - Walking tenths in the left hand.

Listening to master stride pianists reveals how convincingly they create this illusion of two separate, interweaving voices. It is difficult to capture this dynamic interplay in words because it involves both harmonic structure and rhythmic feel, producing a sound that feels like more than just one person playing. I encourage you to listen to solo piano performances by Art Tatum, Teddy Wilson, Oscar Peterson, and other stride masters to get an idea of what I'm trying to explain here.

Stride does not always need to be played at a high speed. It also is an appropriate and effective technique for slow ballad solo piano playing. When playing at slower tempos, it often is desirable to include additional harmonic content in the left hand. In the example of the walking tenths from E^b to A^b, it might look like Figure 4.14.

The chords in this example are all quite large and require an even greater hand span to be able to include the additional notes that fill in each chord.

ADDITIONAL HURDLES IN JAZZ PIANO

We've only scratched the surface in exploring the wide chords commonly used in solo jazz piano. The range of possible patterns and voicings is virtually limitless. My intention here has been to offer a brief overview, just to highlight the typical size of these chords and to illustrate how frequently they appear in jazz playing. As Jeremy Siskind writes in *Playing Solo Jazz Piano,* "For better or worse, tenths are a non-negotiable part of serious solo jazz piano."[12] He softens that harsh reality by providing advice and options for those with smaller hands, but in the end the options he is able to offer restrict the small-handed soloist to performing a simplified, inferior version of the music.

---

[12] Siskind, 2020, p. 13

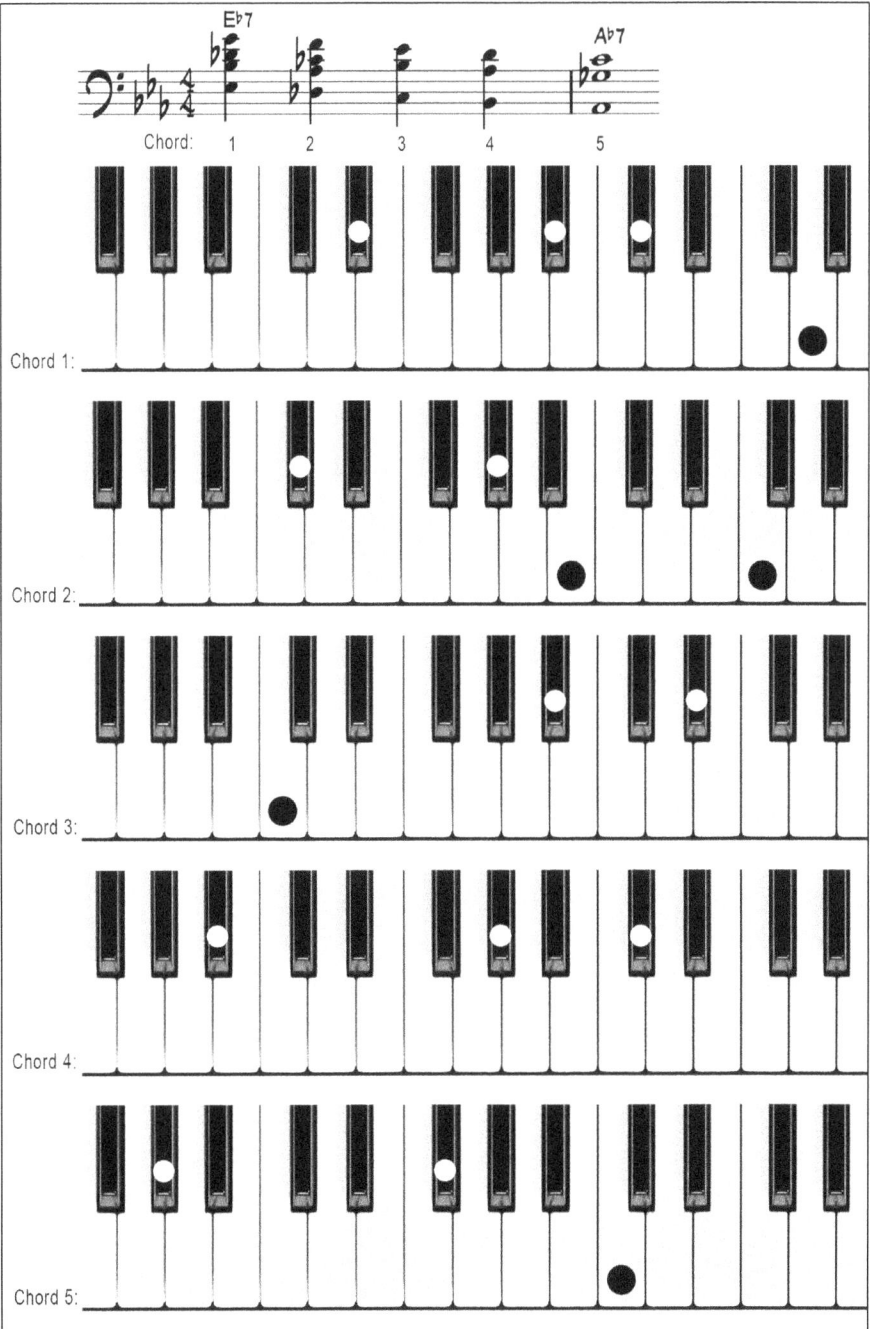

Figure 4.14 - Filled-in walking tenths in the left hand.

These challenges are most evident for jazz soloists, but they also extend to playing in a trio or other group. Let's look at two examples.

Fast Runs, Arpeggios, and Leaps

Fast runs and arpeggios can be more difficult for small-handed pianists if the required fingerings force the hand into stretched or awkward positions. Difficulties arise primarily when the music demands rapid movement across a wide range of keys or incorporates large leaps.

Leaps and jumps are particularly challenging because small hands must move more than large hands to cover the same distance, reducing accuracy and increasing fatigue. Maintaining precision during jumps also is harder, and there is a higher likelihood of missing notes or producing uneven sound. In the most extreme cases, you almost feel like you have to fling your arm across the keyboard and just pray that you land on the right keys.

In transcribing some of Oscar Peterson's playing, I have often found that many of his runs feel unnatural for me to play on a conventional keyboard. They demand excessive stretching, large leaps, or awkward hand positions–techniques that aren't comfortable for me. Yet when Oscar played them, they sounded completely effortless. Part of that, of course, was due to his extraordinary technical skill. But even if I practiced those kinds of phrases until I could execute them cleanly, they would still feel physically uncomfortable and cumbersome on the conventional keyboard. Oscar, on the other hand, not only made them sound effortless, but also entirely unforced. He communicated not just the technical mastery required to play such phrases, but also the spontaneity of true improvisation–as if the phrase, even if never played before, simply flowed out of him. A large part of that ease likely came from the large size of his hands, which made such passages feel natural and physically accessible to him.

Shout Choruses

One arrangement technique often employed in jazz piano trio and quartet pieces is the shout chorus. In big band arrangements, a shout chorus is a high-energy, climactic section in which the entire ensemble typically plays together in a powerful, unified manner. It often serves as the musical peak of a chart, usually appearing about two-thirds of the way through a piece or near the end. It is characterized in several ways. All sections of the band typically play together, often at a loud dynamic. The shout chorus frequently develops or reinterprets earlier melodic material, motifs, or harmonies from the arrangement, sometimes introducing new ideas as well. Melodies are often harmonized in thick block chords in which different sections of the band double or extend each other's lines, creating a rich, full sound. The shout chorus is a signature moment in big band jazz, designed to showcase the ensemble's power and bring the arrangement to an exciting climax.[13]

In a small group or solo piano setting, the shout chorus is often used to drive the piece to its climax, just as it would in a big band arrangement. In these moments, the pianist takes on the role of the full horn section, mimicking the power and energy of a big band shout chorus. Creating this effect places significant physical demands on the player, particularly on the right hand, which typically plays continuous, filled-in octave chords during the shout chorus. The left hand, by contrast, usually plays more manageable voicings, spanning intervals from a fourth to a seventh. Figure 4.15 on the next page is an example of two-handed chords that could be played during the shout chorus of "Satin Doll." The piano diagram only shows the right hand because the left hand is only playing chords within a sixth interval at most. This type of chord voicing could be repeated as often as every eighth note or even in triplets during the shout chorus.

---

[13] Rogers, Evans. "The Shout Chorus." *Big Band Arranging,* https://www.evanrogersmusic.com/blog-contents/big-band-arranging/the-shout-chorus. Accessed July 14, 2025.

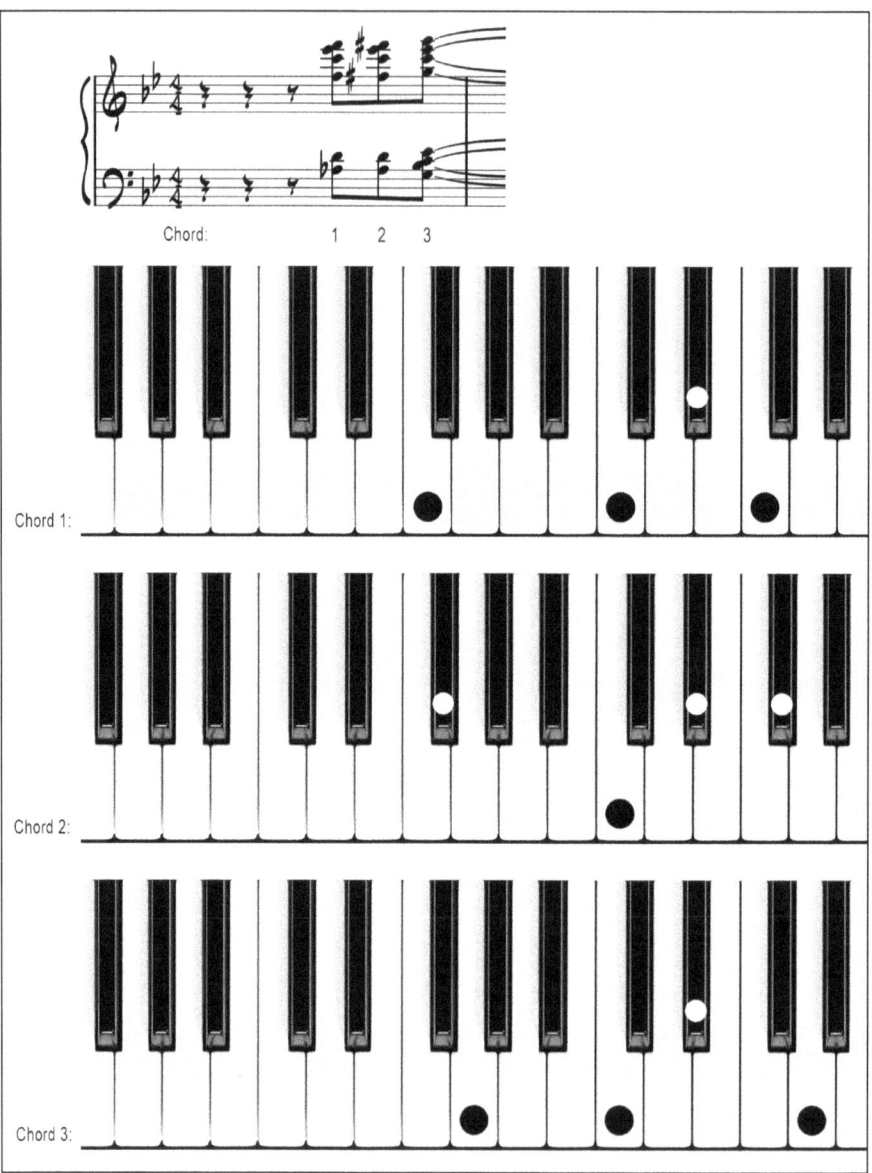

Figure 4.15 - Shout chorus filled-in octave chords in the right hand.

Like its big band counterpart, the small group shout chorus is characterized by loud, energetic, rhythmic block chords such as in this example, often with doubling in octaves (the right hand here) and tight harmonic movement. For small-handed pianists, this kind of passage presents serious challenges in terms of reach, endurance, and hand positioning. The repeated octave chords can quickly lead to fatigue, especially when played at high volume and tempo.

To manage these difficulties, small-handed players must rely on precise technique, strategic hand angle adjustments, selective voicing, and sometimes omitting or redistributing notes to preserve both musical integrity and physical health.

For me, endurance is the hardest part. I can reach all of these chords on the conventional keyboard–even the filled-in octave chords are well within my span–but sustaining them for an entire shout chorus or two is a major strain. As the shout chorus progresses, I can feel the tension and pain building in my hand and forearm. When it finally ends, I have to shake my hand out quickly to get some relief–and the tune still isn't over!

COMPARING HAND SIZES

All of the jazz piano techniques I've discussed–shared-hand voicings, stride piano, fast runs, arpeggios and leaps, and shout choruses–place significant demands on a pianist's hand span. With dedicated practice–often far more than what a larger-handed pianist might require–it is possible to develop a degree of proficiency with some of these techniques. Others may be technically playable, but they come at a cost: they can cause pain, strain, and increase the risk of injury if used too frequently, without sufficient recovery, or with improper form. And then there are the techniques of jazz piano that are simply physically impossible for the small-handed pianist, no matter how much effort is applied.

All of these techniques were heavily employed by Oscar Peterson, and so I had a great desire to be able to master them. Let's now compare Oscar's hands to my own.

In Chapter 6, we will see how hand spans can be broken into four zones from A to D of increasing size. Oscar Peterson's hands fall in Zone D, the largest zone, and this is the zone for which the conventional piano keyboard is optimally sized. While my hands are slightly smaller than the average for males, Oscar Peterson's hands–among the largest of anyone–enabled him to perform techniques that would be difficult for most players, even those with average-sized hands.

There are no published, precise measurements of Oscar Peterson's hand span, however there is sufficient evidence to come to a reasonable estimate. We know Oscar could play all the tenth intervals effortlessly and with great speed when desired. In an interview with the great conductor, composer, and pianist André Previn, Oscar mentioned that he could play filled-in eleventh chords easily,[14] and that would indicate he could also play a twelfth interval if needed.

Based on this information, it is reasonable to assume that Oscar Peterson's hand span from pinky to thumb was between 9.5 inches at the bare minimum and 10 inches or more, with the most likely value in the higher end of this range. My hand spans just over 8 inches. Using these measurements, let's take a look at Oscar's hands and my hands on a conventional keyboard in Figures 4.16 and 4.17.

These diagrams highlight the large difference in span between Oscar Peterson's hands and my own. My hands are playing a ninth interval, which is the limit of my reach. I can just touch the tenths, but they are not playable. In contrast, Oscar Peterson's hands fit comfortably over the eleventh interval, which means he could play all the tenths with ease. Next to Oscar's hands, mine look like a child's hands!

---

[14] BBC Four, "Oscar Peterson Interview with André Previn part 5." *YouTube*, uploaded by @another_bites_the_crust_pizzas_uk, February 19, 2008, https://www.youtube.com/watch?v=u2cyoI-mRiw.

Figure 4.16 - Estimated span of Oscar Peterson's hands on conventional keyboard.

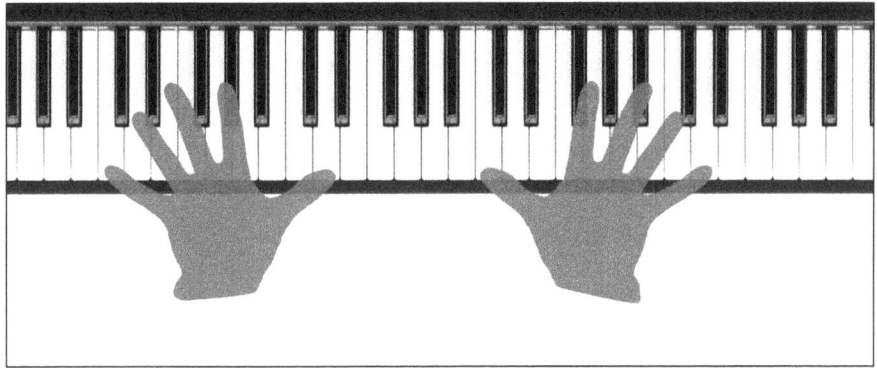

Figure 4.17 - Estimated span of my hands on conventional keyboard.

SEARCHING FOR A SOLUTION

As I struggled to contend with the limitations imposed on me by my smaller hand size, I searched for ways to overcome them. First, I tried shifting notes between hands. As long as everything was within a ninth interval, that worked, but that was rarely the case. As discussed earlier, the problem is that it is very common to find that the desired note you are trying to include requires either the left hand or the right hand to stretch to a tenth, so switching it to the other hand won't help.

Another solution I tried was using hand stretches to increase my hand span. If I could increase my span just a little bit, I could play some of the smaller tenth intervals, such as black to black key tenths. I did not achieve much with these efforts.

At the height of my frustration, I even attached a homemade extender to my left pinky. After experimenting with various shapes made of cardboard and tape, I found that I could reasonably play tenth intervals in my left hand.

The extender did allow me to create some of the sounds I wanted, and for a time I worked with it. But this was a clumsy solution, forcing me to adjust my technique. It did not allow me to have full control, it limited my speed, and I lacked power when playing tenths. Additionally, I was unable to apply the same approach to my right hand because the right hand is significantly more active while playing. As a result, these issues would be even more pronounced, making it virtually impossible to perform with any fluidity.

The absurdity of my cardboard and tape extender only underscored the problem of my small hand size. My frustration with what seemed to be an insurmountable difficulty was beginning to make me lose motivation for my jazz piano studies.

Chapter 5

COMMON-SENSE SOLUTION

The Innovation of Narrower Keyboards

The solution to my difficulties with the conventional keyboard was actually quite simple. I can't change the size of my hands, but what if I could change the size of my piano keys? If each key were narrower, I would suddenly be able to play larger intervals with ease, even those I had not been able to reach at all on a conventional keyboard.

It seems so obvious, yet the conventional size of the piano keyboard has remained unchanged for nearly 150 years, becoming so deeply embedded in tradition that most people never question whether the keys might be too wide for many players. As a result, alternative narrower key sizes have rarely even been considered.

This idea is far from new, however. In fact, among advocates for narrower piano keyboards, it is well-known that the renowned concert pianist Josef Hofmann (1876-1957) played on a Steinway piano fitted with a custom, slightly narrower keyboard made by

Steinway & Sons to better suit his hands, which were smaller than the average male's hands.[15]

Josef Hofmann began his musical career as a child prodigy and became a performer of international renown. He was mentored by Anton Rubinstein and held the position of director at the Curtis Institute of Music. His inventive spirit was notable. He held more than sixty patents across several fields. Hofmann's inventions include shock absorbers, a spring-loaded car bumper, and windshield wipers inspired by the movement of a metronome. His contributions to piano technology included the invention of the height-adjustable piano bench, pedal extensions for shorter players, and experimentation with improving piano sound for recording and amplification.[16] Most notably, Hoffman had two Steinway pianos made in the 1930s with slightly narrower keys, which he found more comfortable for his smaller hands.[17]

Josef Hofmann is an early example of a pianist who was able to challenge the tradition of the universal piano keyboard. Of course, the reality is that a piano is a complex, substantial instrument to build, requiring significant time and expense. Historically, it simply wasn't practical for manufacturers to produce keyboards in different sizes for the general public, and Hofmann's innovative keyboards remained limited to his own use and did not influence mainstream piano production. But in 1991, a chance encounter between two ambitious and inventive men sparked an idea that would make interchangeable keyboards, customizable for any piano, a real possibility.

---

[15] "Josef Hofmann." *Steinway & Sons,* https://www.steinway.com/artists/josef-hofmann. Accessed July 16, 2025.
[16] "Josef Hofmann – The Pianist Inventor." *Piano Street Magazine,* https://www.pianostreet.com/blog/articles/josef-hofmann-the-pianist-inventor-13049/. Accessed August 19, 2025.
[17] "New Standard for Smaller Piano Keyboards." *LivingPianos,* https://livingpianos.com/standart-smaller-keyboards. Accessed August 19, 2025.

CHRISTOPHER DONISON AND DAVID STEINBUHLER

The first of these men is Christopher Donison, a Canadian pianist and composer who struggled with his piano studies for years due to the small size of his hands. One day he had a revelation that rather than his hands being too small, the keys were too wide. That gave him the idea–you guessed it–to pursue a piano keyboard with narrower keys.[18]

The inspiration for this idea came to him while practicing a Chopin ballade in the early 1970s. After years of believing that his hands were simply too small, he began to wonder if, in fact, the problem was that the keyboard was too big. Donison recognized that in order to reach this kind of insight, you have to be willing to question what you have always been told, and allow your imagination to move beyond conventional boundaries. He notes that if you've spent your entire life with only one universal piano keyboard, it's easy to presume that's the only possibility. When he first shared his idea with others, many dismissed it–not because there was any logical reason not to accept it, but because it went against a deeply ingrained norm that they had never thought to question.[19]

Donison, like Hofmann before him, refused to accept the conventional keyboard, and he worked with piano technicians and engineers to build a narrower keyboard for his own piano. Like the specialty keyboards Steinway built for Hofmann, Donison's narrower keyboard was a unique, custom design.

But Donison realized many more pianists than just himself would benefit from having narrower keyboards available. He began to believe that the world should embrace a second, officially recognized keyboard size, available universally for practice, performance, and competitions. However, he worried that not every piano could be modified to fit this new standard.[20]

---

[18] Donison, Christopher. "DS Keyboard." *Christopher Donison,* http://www.chrisdonison.com/keyboard.html. Accessed July 16, 2025.
[19] Ibid.
[20] Ibid.

In the summer of 1991, Donison ran a bed and breakfast while he was serving as Music Director at the Shaw Festival in Niagara-on-the-Lake, Ontario. One of his guests happened to be David Steinbuhler, a man with the skills and resources needed to turn Donison's idea into a reality. Donison discussed his idea with Steinbuhler.[21] He explained to Steinbuhler that for this idea to succeed, a business entity would be needed to lead the way and provide conversions to the alternate standard for any piano. This would require an advanced computer program to accurately cut keys and build a database for manufacturing custom replacement keyboards suitable for any instrument. Steinbuhler expressed confidence that he could develop such a program, and he had all the equipment necessary to make the keyboards in his family's textile factory in Titusville, Pennsylvania.[22]

About a week after this meeting, Donison received a visit from an old friend and fellow Canadian, Linda Gould, a pianist, author, and educator originally from Calgary. Gould began her music career at age eleven with a performance alongside the Mount Royal College orchestra and has performed and taught internationally for over 40 years. She first met Christopher Donison during their university years, where the two quickly bonded. They often commiserated over the difficulty their smaller hands posed at the piano, even joking about how they wished they could simply trade them in for larger ones.[23]

That week after the Shaw Festival in 1991, Gould was on a business trip near Donison's home and took the opportunity to reconnect with her friend and to try out Donison's narrower keyboard. During their visit, the two pianists revived their old discussion about narrow keys. Donison told Gould about his meeting with Steinbuhler, and together they decided to contact Steinbuhler to see if he would be willing to build a prototype.[24]

---

[21] The 1991 meeting date is according to David Steinbuhler (https://dsstandardfoundation.org/the-standards/#ourstory). Donison recalls this meeting taking place in 1993. That may refer to a related event rather than their initial meeting. Most sources that discuss this meeting place it in 1991.

[22] Donison, "DS Keyboard."

[23] Email correspondence with Linda Gould, August 25, 2025; Topham, Tim, "The Narrow Key Piano Crusade with Linda Gould and Rhonda Boyle." *YouTube,* uploaded by @TopMusicCo - Tim Topham, December 10, 2023.

[24] Email correspondence, August 25, 2025.

It turned out Steinbuhler had been considering the project all week. As an inventor, he was drawn to the challenge, and he was particularly motivated by the impact it could have on the musical world.[25]

THE TECHNICAL CHALLENGES

With no preconceptions about piano manufacturing, Steinbuhler began experimenting in his family's textile plant, which was equipped with all the machinery he needed to cut keys and assemble a piano keyboard, such as a CNC (computer numeric control) router, which is used in piano manufacturing and other industries to shape wooden parts with high accuracy and consistency. He developed a prototype keyboard and installed it in a Steinway upright.

The keyboard was far from perfect. Steinbuhler identified several issues resulting from the reduced key width that needed to be resolved before the keyboards could be marketed to the public. Some challenges were structural in nature: the narrower keys experienced increased mechanical stress, raising concerns about the durability of the components and the instrument's ability to withstand rigorous use. Additionally, Steinbuhler sought input from pianists to evaluate any alterations in the keyboard's touch and playability, as his goal was for the narrower keyboards to replicate the feel of conventional ones.

The first professional to try Steinbuhler's prototype was Linda Gould. Gould recognized the breakthrough in technology that Steinbuhler had already achieved and the tremendous benefit it offered her, despite the deficiencies of the prototype. Gould recalls:

> *My passion for narrow keys goes back almost 30 years. I injured my hand in my 20s and thought serious piano playing was over for me. Then, thanks to Chris Donison and David Steinbuhler, I tried a narrow-key prototype. The very first time I touched it, everything changed. Suddenly I could play for hours without pain. I could perform again. That moment gave me back the piano… better than it was before.[26]*

---

[25] Donison, "DS Keyboard."
[26] Email correspondence, August 20, 2025.

She immediately became Steinbuhler's first customer and ordered a keyboard for her Yamaha grand. As she relates, "David had done a brilliant job. I'll never forget trying it for the first time–I ordered one on the spot, with tears in my eyes."[27]

At that point, Steinbuhler shifted his attention to building keyboards for grand pianos and addressing the technical problems of narrower keyboards his prototype had uncovered.[28]

The challenges were formidable but not insurmountable for someone of Steinbuhler's skill and craftsmanship. Obviously, the main task was to make the keys narrower, but you can't just cut thinner pieces of wood and expect the piano to function as before. Narrower keys have a trickle-down effect on the construction of the entire instrument. Steinbuhler had a complex engineering problem on his hands. He had to completely re-design the piano keys. Because the keys were to become narrower, they would not be as strong as normal piano keys. When played, these thinner keys would be more likely to bend and twist, especially if they were pushed down harder while playing. On a conventional piano keyboard, the keys are thick enough to resist these stresses, but on a smaller keyboard, Steinbuhler found the keys feel softer, almost "spongy," and don't bounce back as quickly.[29]

When modifying a regular piano to have a keyboard with narrower keys, most of the keys are shifted so that the playable end of each key no longer aligns correctly with the internal workings of the rest of the action. As illustrated in Figures 5.1 and 5.2, while the overall width of the keyboard's playing surface becomes narrower, the interior of the action–where the hammers strike the strings–remains the same width. This offset increases as you move away from the center of the keyboard and is largest and most noticeable for the keys at the extreme high and low ends of the keyboard. The increasing offset requires an increasing angle of bend in the keys, or key flare, to keep the back end of the keys aligned with their hammers and strings.[30]

---

[27] Email correspondence, August 25, 2025.

[28] Steinbuhler, David. "The DS Standard." *Standard Foundation,* https://dsstandardfoundation.org/the-standards/#story. Accessed July 16, 2025.

[29] Steinbuhler, David (1998). Stiffened Key (U.S. Patent No. 5,847,301). U.S. Patent and Trademark Office.

[30] Ibid.

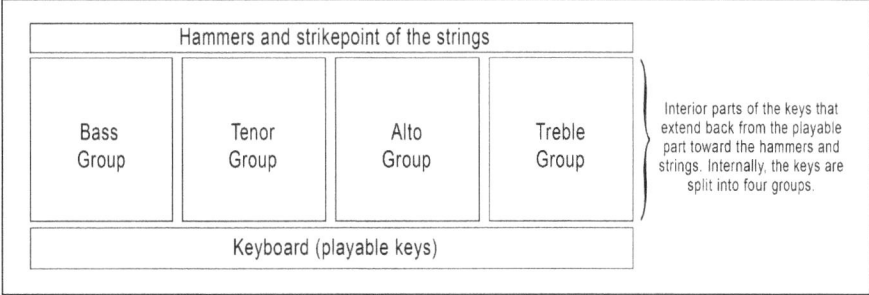

Figure 5.1 - Conceptual diagram of piano keys showing how they connect from the playable part to the hammers and strings on a conventional keyboard.

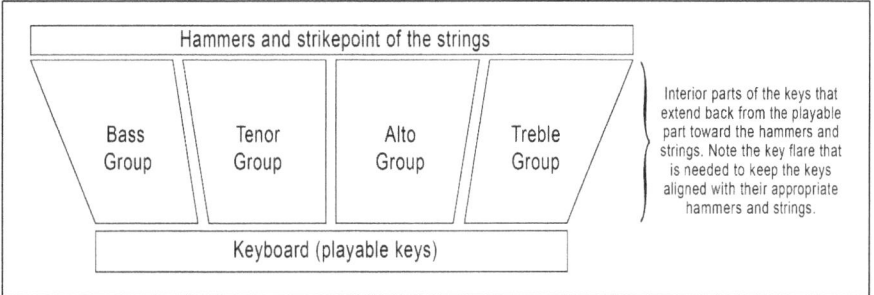

Figure 5.2 - Conceptual diagram of piano keys showing the key flare required to keep the keys of a narrower keyboard aligned with the hammers and strings at the back of the action.

All these changes make narrower keys less firm and not as responsive as what pianists are used to. As a result, Steinbuhler needed to find a way to make narrow keys that still feel strong and springy, so the piano feels and plays as well as one with a conventional keyboard.[31]

The solution Steinbuhler settled on was to introduce a bracing member to each key. Normally, a key is one continuous piece of wood from the part your fingers strike all the way to the back of the key, which connects to the capstan mechanism that then causes the hammer to strike the strings. Steinbuhler created three different designs for the construction of a key with a bracing member.[32]

---

[31] Ibid.
[32] Ibid.

We'll look at two of the options, which will be sufficient to understand how the bracing member resolves the structural challenges of the narrower keys. Figure 5.3 shows a conventional piano key. Note that it is a single, continuous piece of wood.

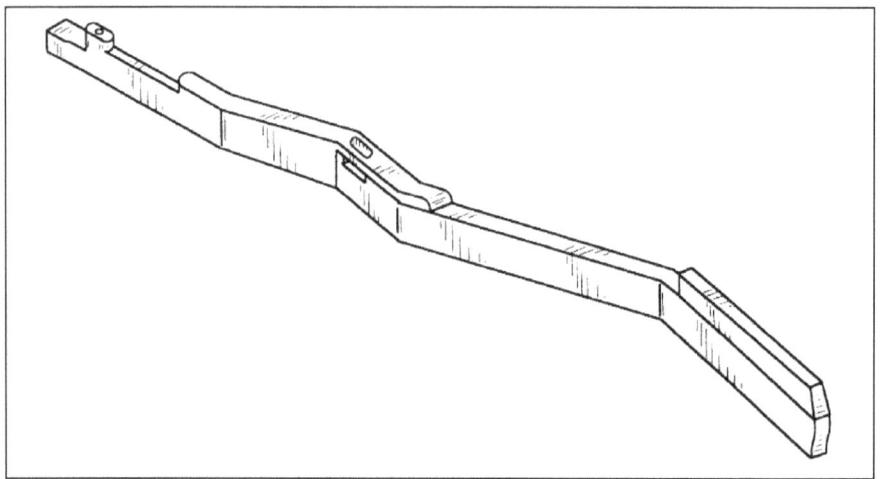

Figure 5.3 - Conventional piano key. From Steinbuhler, David (1998). Stiffened Key (U.S. Patent No. 5,847,301). U.S. Patent and Trademark Office.

The first option Steinbuhler proposed was to construct the key in three separate pieces–the part you play, the bracing member, and the key shank, which is the internal part of the key that connects it to the rest of the action. With this option, the bracing member is mounted below both the playing member and the key shank, and it provides the necessary additional strength and resistance to twisting and flexing. In Figure 5.4, element 7 is the playable part of the key (a black key), element 16 is the key shank, and element 2 is the bracing element.[33]

The second option maintains the continuity between the playable part of the key and the key shank by introducing a connecting member that bridges the gap caused by the increased flare of the keys. In Figure 5.5, element 7 is the playable part of the key (again a black key), element 6 is the key shank, element 20 is the connecting member between the playable part of the key and the key shank, and element 2 is the bracing element.[34]

---

[33] Ibid.
[34] Ibid.

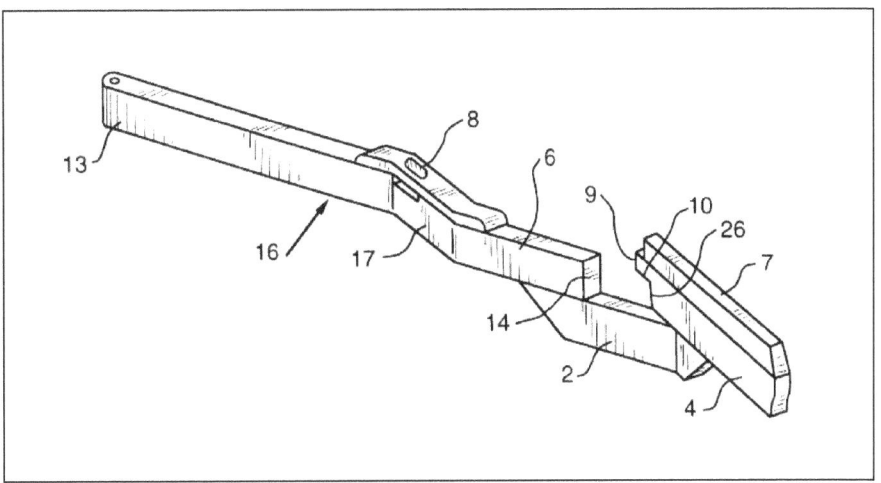

Figure 5.4 - Stiffened piano key, option 1. From Steinbuhler, David (1998). Stiffened Key (U.S. Patent No. 5,847,301). U.S. Patent and Trademark Office.

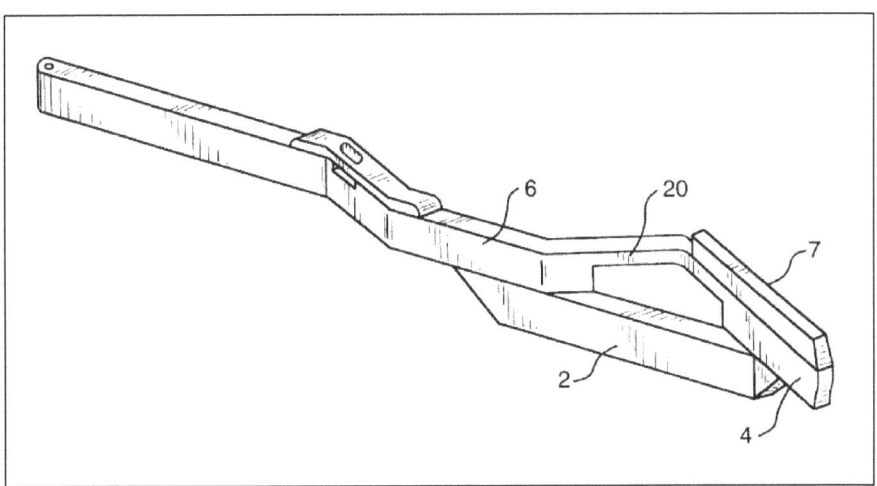

Figure 5.5 - Stiffened piano key, option 2. From Steinbuhler, David (1998). Stiffened Key (U.S. Patent No. 5,847,301). U.S. Patent and Trademark Office.

In both of these options, Steinbuhler had to ensure that the reinforced keys could be placed next to each other and still work properly. There needs to be enough space so that pressing one key doesn't touch or affect its neighbor. As seen in Figures 5.6 and 5.7, Steinbuhler trimmed away a portion of the underside at the back of the key–the part that sits below the section the player touches. By thinning this portion of the key and creating more empty space, the key can move downward freely without its underside colliding with the key next to it. In addition, a small gap must be maintained between the rear edge of the key top and the front portion of the internal structure of the adjacent key. This space helps prevent binding or unwanted contact during normal key movement. Additionally, room must be left so that when you push a key down, the bottom of any connecting piece doesn't hit the support piece of the neighboring key. This extra space is usually made by keeping the connecting piece from being too thick vertically. Steinbuhler fulfilled all these requirements in his design.[35]

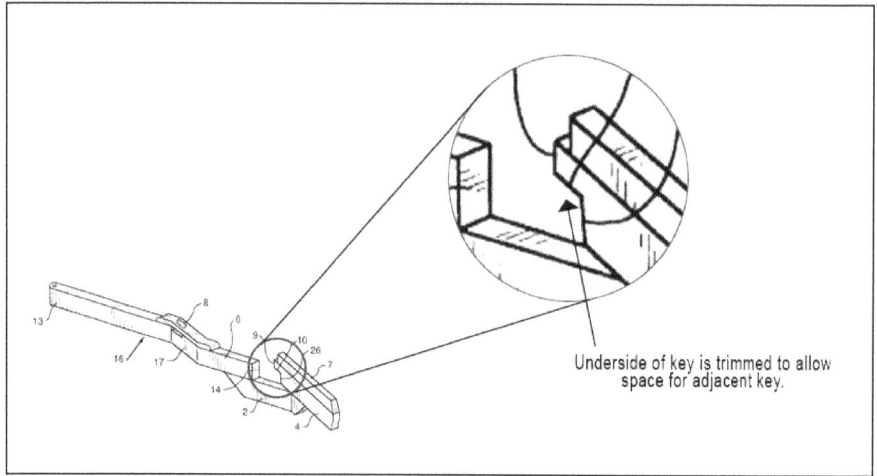

Figure 5.6 - Detail of option 1, showing trimmed space that prevents collision with the adjacent key. Adapted from Steinbuhler, David (1998). Stiffened Key (U.S. Patent No. 5,847,301). U.S. Patent and Trademark Office.

One problem with the bracing element is that it adds weight and bulk to the keys. The bracing element is especially needed at the extreme ends of the keyboard–in the low bass notes and high treble notes–because at these locations the offset of the key from its position on the conventional keyboard is maximum, and a greater level of key flare, i.e., a greater angle of bend in the key, is needed to align the back of the key with the rest of the action as we illustrated conceptually in Figures 5.1 and 5.2. Figure 5.8 shows what the key flare looks like on a full set of 88 piano keys. In the bass, the extra weight of the bracing elements is not as much of an issue because the player is used to the bass keys being heavier and requiring more force to play. But in the

---

[35] Ibid.

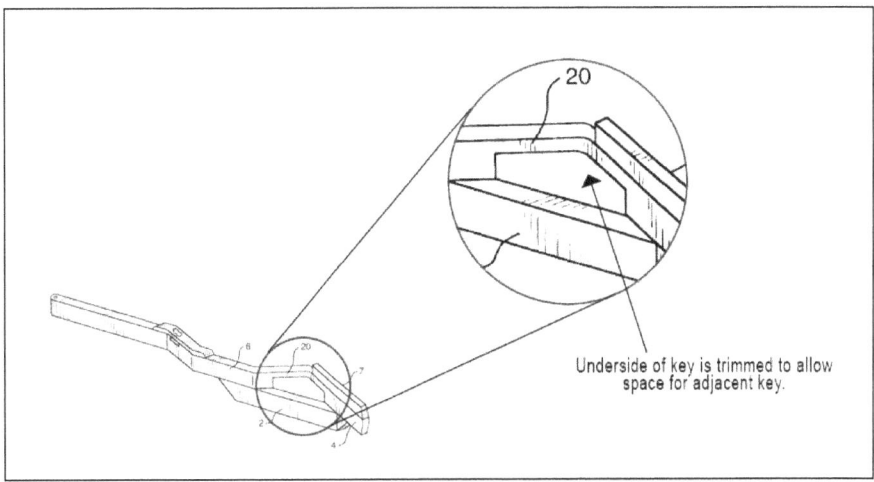

Figure 5.7 - Detail of option 2, showing trimmed space that prevents collision with the adjacent key. Adapted from Steinbuhler, David (1998). Stiffened Key (U.S. Patent No. 5,847,301). U.S. Patent and Trademark Office.

upper treble section, the problem is most apparent because the player expects those keys to have a lighter touch. The more the width of the keyboard is reduced from the conventional width, the more pronounced is this effect due to the increased level of key flare and consequent higher level of bracing that is needed.[36]

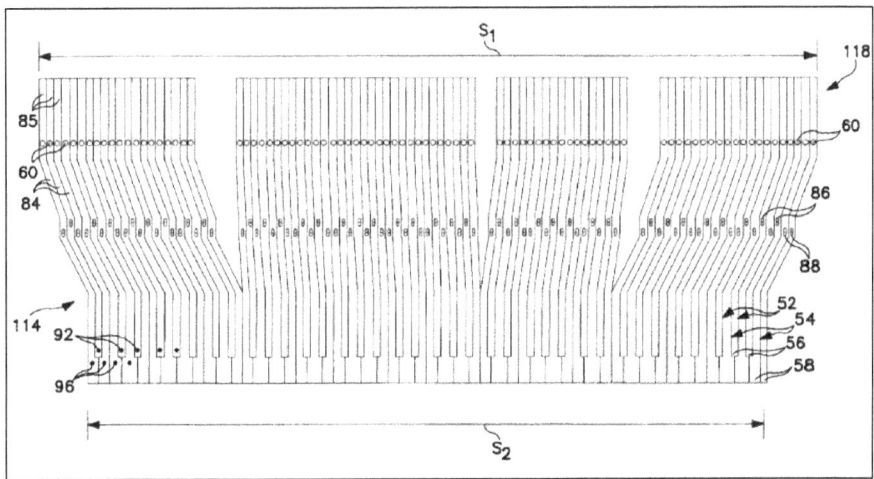

Figure 5.8 - Modified grand piano keyboard. From Steinbuhler, David (2000). Reduced-Size Keyboards (U.S. Patent No. 6,118,063). U.S. Patent and Trademark Office.

[36] Steinbuhler, David (2000). Reduced-Size Keyboards (U.S. Patent No. 6,118,063). U.S. Patent and Trademark Office.

Steinbuhler suggested two ways to mitigate this problem. First, the keyboard could be designed so that the long part of some of the highest or lowest keys (i.e. the key shank) is angled in a way that the bend is closer to the front of the keyboard than is normally done. As illustrated in Figure 5.9, moving the initiation of the key flare forward both decreases the angle of the key flare and increases the thickness of the key shank, which increases the overall stability of the key. This approach means that sometimes part of the bend in a key might stick out in front of the fall board, which normally hides the back part of the keys from the player's sight. The bend in the upper keys would be visible to the player, but this solution would reduce or even eliminate the need for the bracing elements.

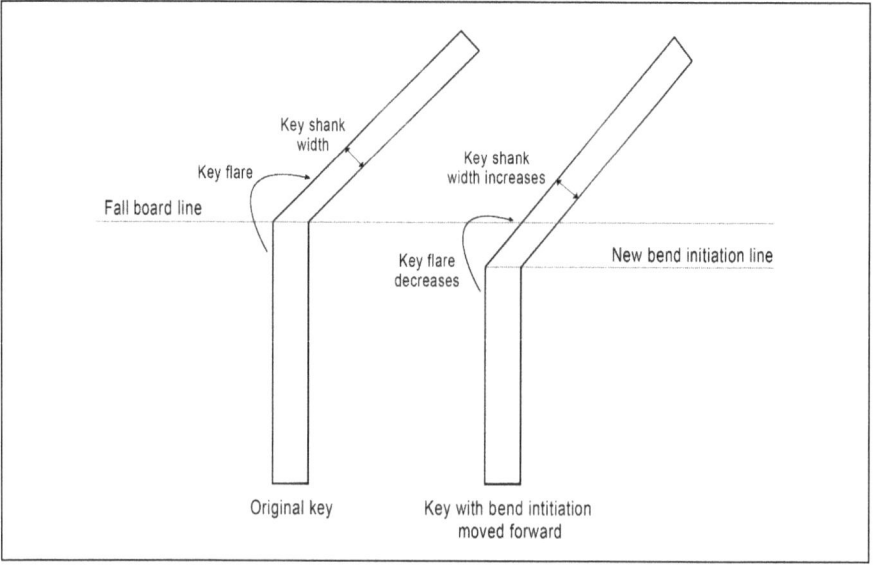

Figure 5.9 - By moving the initiation of the key flare forward, its angle is reduced, and the key shank can be made slightly thicker.

Figure 5.10 illustrates how the bend in the keys is visible to the player. The imaginary line H indicates where the fall board would normally be. The first keys on the left of the diagram line up with the fall board as on a conventional keyboard, but as you move toward the right to the extreme end of the keyboard, the initiation of the bend occurs earlier, and the key bend would therefore be visible to the player.[37]

---

[37] Ibid.

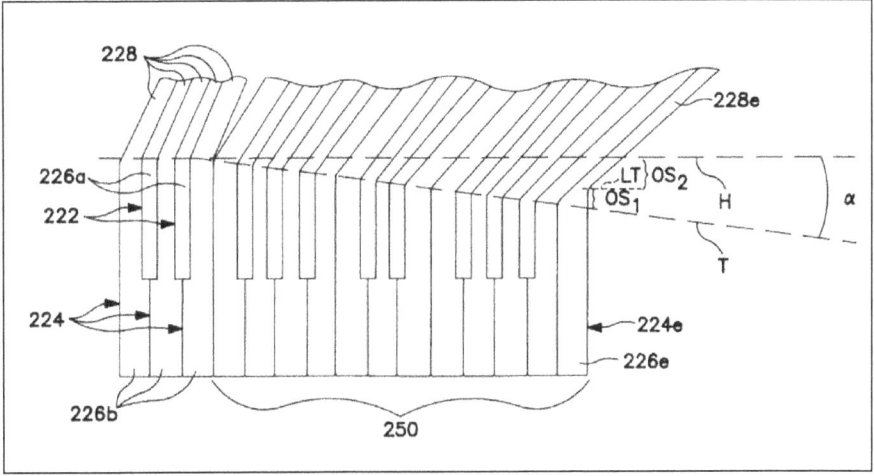

Figure 5.10 - Moving the key bend forward. From Steinbuhler, David (2000). Reduced-Size Keyboards (U.S. Patent No. 6,118,063). U.S. Patent and Trademark Office.

This first option works well in the upper treble section where it is desirable to eliminate the bracing elements completely to maintain a lighter touch in the keys. A second option may be better for the lower bass keys, where a heavier touch is desired and the bracing elements are needed for stability, but reducing their added weight through other modifications allows finer control over the key's feel. The principle here is similar to the first option, but instead of the key bend moving forward toward the front of the key, the bracing element is extended further toward the front of the piano than is typical, which decreases the angle of the key flare and allows the key shank to be thicker and more stable. The support bar itself might also be angled, potentially requiring an indent or cutout in the piano case to fit it in.[38]

Figure 5.11 on the next page shows a bottom-up view of the bass section of the piano where the observer is underneath the keyboard looking up at it, so the far bass is on the right side of the figure, and the more central area of the keyboard is on the left side of the figure. The bottom of the figure represents the front side of the piano. Element 300 is the front rail of the piano. Element 304 is

---

[38] Ibid.

the midrail further back in the piano. Elements 310 and 310e are the (bottom side of the) bracing elements, and F is an imaginary line that represents where the front rail would end on the unmodified piano. The rail has been cut into so that the bracing elements can be extended forward. Note that this means the initiation of the bend in the bracing element is occurring closer to the front of the key, which allows them to be lighter in weight while providing the same amount of stability. Also, since the bracing element is located below the visible part of the key, the player does not see any visible bend in the key as they do with the first option.[39]

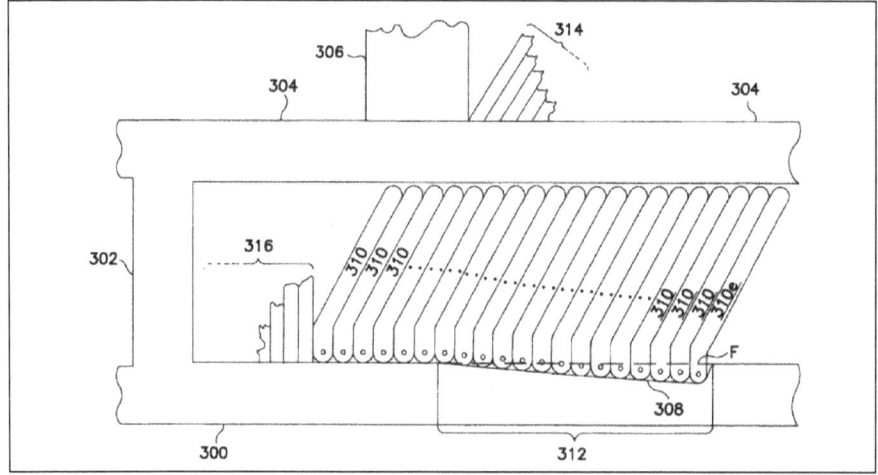

Figure 5.11 - Extending the bracing members. From Steinbuhler, David (2000). Reduced-Size Keyboards (U.S. Patent No. 6,118,063). U.S. Patent and Trademark Office.

These additional adjustments are needed most for the more extreme changes in keyboard width, for example the DS5.1. Steinbuhler also contemplated an even narrower keyboard at roughly 4.85 inches per octave, and these additional elements of the design would be critical at that size, which otherwise would be impossible to attain.[40]

What does this look like in actual practice? Figure 5.12 shows a DS5.1 keyboard installed in David Steinbuhler's own piano, which I

---

[39] Ibid.
[40] Ibid.

had a chance to play in Titusville in 2023 (see Chapter 8). The fall board is not in place on the piano, which enables you to see the shank part of the keys, which would normally be hidden from the player's view. It is clear that if the fall board were in place, the bend of the keys in the upper treble section would be visible to the player as highlighted in the circled area in Figure 5.12. The playable parts of the keys clearly reveal the bend in the keys. In the bass, the bend is not visible to the player, indicating that Steinbuhler opted for the second option in the bass. Further, we can see that the flare angle is greater in the bass notes than in the treble notes, making the second option more desirable since the bracing elements are still in place with that option.

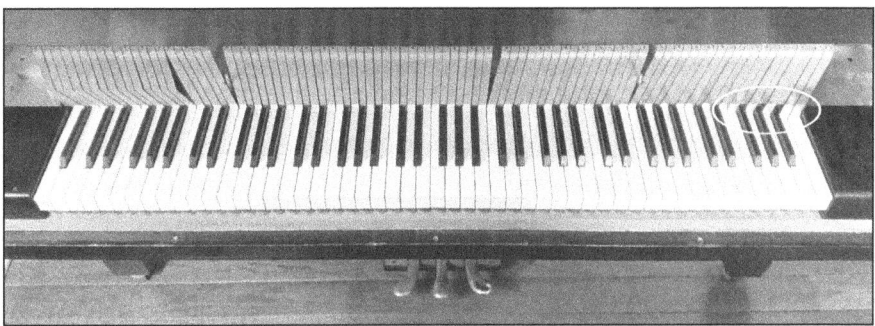

Figure 5.12 - David Steinbuhler's piano fitted with a DS5.1 keyboard. Note the key flare would be visible to the player in the high treble section (circled area).[41]

STEINBUHLER'S KEYBOARDS

To facilitate demonstrations and academic studies, Steinbuhler developed technician-adjustable keyboards that could be mounted in various instruments, allowing music institutions such as schools and concert halls to provide both conventional and narrower keyboards interchangeably without modifying the pianos. He even developed a custom tool kit for piano technicians to use in making their measurements and precise adjustments for each piano.[42]

---

[41] Photograph by the author.
[42] Steinbuhler, David. "The DS Standard." *Standard Foundation,* https://dsstandardfoundation.org/the-standards/#story. Accessed July 16, 2025.

During my visit to Titusville, I observed Steinbuhler swapping the actions in and out of his piano. It took only a minute or two to complete each replacement because the actions had already been finely adjusted for his piano. It would take a technician a little longer to swap out the action for the first time, but the process is quite simple in any case.

Steinbuhler developed two options for his keyboards. The first option involves building and installing a completely new action, including new wippens and hammers. In a piano action, each key has a wippen and a hammer. The wippen acts as an intermediate lever that helps transfer the movement of pressing a key to raising the hammer, which strikes the string. The wippen is also essential to the double escapement system, which ensures the hammer can fall back freely immediately after striking the string, even if the key has not yet been released. This system allows for playing rapidly repeated notes.[43]

Because all these parts are new, the piano's sound will change. It won't sound exactly like the original piano, as new hammers in particular have a large impact on tone. The benefit, however, is that the new action can be swapped with the original action/keyboard quickly, so it is possible to alternate between the new and original size as desired. This option is ideal for large performances such as concerts, which might require quick changes between set-ups.[44]

The second option uses the original action stack (the original hammers and wippens) but places it on a new frame with the new keyboard. Since the original hammers and other action parts are retained, the piano's original sound character is preserved completely. Here's the drawback of this option: although a technician can restore the action back to its original configuration, it won't be a quick process.[45]

---

[43] "Wippen." *Britannica*, https://www.britannica.com/art/wippen. Accessed August 20, 2025.
[44] Steinbuhler, David. "Products." *Standard Foundation*, https://dsstandardfoundation.org/products/. Accessed July 17, 2025.
[45] Ibid.

The Standards

David Steinbuhler pioneered the field of alternative size keyboards. He was the first to build narrower keyboards for acoustic pianos on a larger scale and make them available to the public. Steinbuhler solved all of the technical design challenges that arose, and he committed himself through his DS Standard® Foundation to producing narrower keyboards, raising awareness about the need for and benefits of these keyboards, and making them available to as many people as possible, primarily through loans to music schools.[46]

David Steinbuhler established the Donison-Steinbuhler, or DS Standard® sizes, which are named based on the width of one octave on the keyboard. The standard sizes are:[47]

■ DS6.5 - the conventional size, having 6.5 inches per octave

■ DS6.0® - the "universal" keyboard that may be a more suitable default size, having 6.0 inches per octave

■ DS5.5® - roughly ⅞ size of conventional, having 5.5 inches per octave

■ DS5.1 - primarily intended for children, but also used by some adults (including me), having 5.1 inches per octave

As we'll see in Chapter 8, this set of standard sizes enables the overwhelming majority of people to play the piano as if they had larger hands.

Steinbuhler included even smaller sizes for children. He has not produced these smaller keyboards, but based on the solutions he developed for mitigating the increased structural stresses at the

---

[46] Steinbuhler, David. "About." *Standard Foundation,* https://dsstandardfoundation.org/about/. Accessed July 17, 2025.
[47] Steinbuhler, "The DS Standard®."

extreme ends of highly-reduced width keyboards, these sizes would also be possible:[48]

- DS4.7 - ¾ size of conventional

- DS4.3

- DS4.0 - ⅝ size of conventional

> ## Speaking of Standards
>
> There is no standard way to refer to narrower keyboards. They've been called reduced size keyboards, alternative size keyboards, narrower keyboards, ergonomically scaled piano keyboards (ESPKs), and stretto (Italian for narrow) pianos. In this book I've settled on "narrower keyboards" and sometimes "alternative size" keyboards depending on the context.

DIGITAL INSTRUMENTS

Nearly all of the technical challenges addressed by David Steinbuhler's narrower keyboard design arise from the need to fit a new, smaller keyboard into a piano originally built for the conventional size. Since it's a retrofit system, every component must align perfectly so that the keys trigger the hammers to strike the strings at the correct spots. His design also had to account for the extra physical stress on the keys at the very top and bottom of the keyboard, where the playable parts of the keys are most widely offset from their normal positions.

When it comes to digital instruments, however, many of the mechanical and alignment challenges inherent in acoustic piano design do not apply. Digital piano makers have much more freedom in their designs. They can create keyboards of virtually any shape or size without being constrained by mechanical complexities of hammers and strings.

---

[48] Ibid.

The primary challenge for digital piano designers is ensuring the authentic weight and tactile feel of the keys. Achieving this realistic touch is essential to make the playing experience feel natural and comfortable. Fortunately, designers have a wide range of materials and technologies at their disposal–from weighted key mechanisms and graded hammer actions to innovative materials–that allow them to finely tune the resistance, responsiveness, and overall feel of each key.

With thoughtful engineering and careful selection of materials, digital piano manufacturers can replicate or even customize key action to suit various ergonomic or performance needs. This flexibility means that narrower keyboards are much more feasible in digital instruments, opening new possibilities for accessibility and expressive playing that are more difficult or costly to realize in traditional acoustic pianos.

Despite it being less technically challenging to build narrower digital piano keyboards, it took more than 25 years since David Steinbuhler built his first acoustic retrofit keyboard before digital options began to appear. Major digital piano makers such as Roland, Yamaha, and Casio have been hesitant to offer narrower key options, largely because they doubt there is sufficient market demand. These companies remain tied to the cultural norm of the standard keyboard size, and until strong consumer interest emerges, they are unlikely to change course. This has left room for smaller, more agile startups to take the initiative and begin offering alternatives–a development that is just starting to take shape. Here is an overview of what's available for narrower digital keyboards as of this writing.

Narrow Keys NK 5.5

In 2022, the Narrow Keys company, co-founded by Linda Gould and Kathy Strauch, released the NK 5.5, a digital MIDI[49] keyboard.

---

[49] MIDI stands for Musical Instrument Digital Interface. MIDI keyboards must be connected to a computer or other device that accepts and interprets MIDI signals and converts them to sound.

I bought one of the first 10 commercially available NK 5.5 instruments, my first narrower keyboard.

I found the touch to be very smooth and the keyboard pleasant to play. It is definitely a keyboard–not a piano. It feels like the digital keyboard that it is and not like a real piano action at all. That's to be expected, however, since it is a MIDI controller that uses velocity-based sensors to read the user's physical inputs. Velocity-based sensors work by sensing how quickly or how hard you press a key. They then turn this movement into digital signals that control how loud or soft the sound is and how its tone changes. This ability to detect the speed and force of the player's movements helps create the expressive and dynamic sounds that make digital pianos feel more like real acoustic ones.

One of the features of the instrument is its triple sensors, which allows rapid repetition of notes, similar to what the double escapement mechanism provides on an acoustic action as described earlier. This rapid note repetition works well on the NK 5.5.

The octave size is 5.5 inches. The size proportion of the black to white keys is slightly adjusted so that the black keys are a little bit narrower than they would normally be in the standard DS5.5 size, and this provides some extra space between the black keys for those who have thicker fingers. I have no problem fitting my fingers between the black keys on the NK 5.5 with room to spare.

Athena

Based on the success of the NK 5.5 and feedback from customers, the Narrow Keys company started working on its next instrument, Athena, which started shipping to customers in September 2025.

Athena is a full-featured DS5.5 digital piano keyboard. It features on-board sound and speakers so it can be played as a standalone instrument. It can also be connected to a computer or other device that interprets MIDI data to produce its sound. The graded hammer action makes the instrument feel authentic. Accessories such as a digital piano stand and three-pedal system make the instrument the first complete digital piano available in the DS5.5 size.[50]

Kawai MP11SE Retrofit by David Steinbuhler

The Kawai MP11SE is a premium stage piano highly regarded for its authentic grand piano experience, focusing on both realistic feel and superior sound quality. Its action and key design are among its standout features, appealing to pianists seeking the closest match to an acoustic grand in a digital instrument.

Because the MP11SE has full-length wood keys that have essentially the same design as those found in an acoustic piano, David Steinbuhler is able to use the same technology he developed for acoustic pianos to retrofit a narrower keyboard into the Kawai digital instrument. This retrofit was first requested by pianist and composer Lionel Yu. Yu asked Steinbuhler to retrofit a DS6.0 keyboard into his Kawai MP11SE, which Steinbuhler successfully accomplished.[51]

I have asked David Steinbuhler about retrofitting a DS5.1 keyboard into the Kawai MP11SE. There are technical challenges involved in that extreme retrofit into a digital instrument, which as of the date of this writing Steinbuhler has not yet worked out.

Kaduk Musical Instruments

Kaduk Musical Instruments, founded by Thomas Kaduk, is based in Europe, and they are the only other company I am aware of that offers digital pianos in non-conventional keyboard sizes. We will return to Thomas Kaduk and Kaduk Musical Instruments in Chapter 10, where I describe in detail the custom digital piano they built for me.

But first, let's review research findings and other objective evidence to demonstrate the widespread need for narrower piano keyboards.

---

[50] "Athena." *Narrow Keys,* https://www.narrowkeys.com/athena. Accessed July 17, 2025.
[51] Yu, Lionel, "Piano's Darkest Secret." *YouTube,* uploaded by @MusicalBasics, February 5, 2022, https://www.youtube.com/watch?v=ZXlknI-Jc48.

Chapter 6

NUMBERS TELL THE STORY

*Research on Hand Span and Its
Effect On Pianists*

Given the struggles I've faced in playing the conventional piano keyboard, it's easy to see how the innovation of a narrower keyboard has solved this problem for me. Maybe my personal case is unusual because of the nature of the music I play, containing chords with intervals of unusual size. On the other hand, maybe there are many other people that are having their own difficulties because of their hand size.

The idea of using narrower keyboards has existed for years, yet it still hasn't become mainstream. Does this mean that, as logical as the solution may seem, it isn't as effective or necessary as we might think?

In this chapter, we will review research on hand spans and use it to answer the following two questions:

- How many people require a narrower keyboard in order to play a full repertoire of piano music properly and safely?

- How many people who have hands that are large enough to accommodate the conventional keyboard would nonetheless benefit from having a smaller keyboard, such as the DS6.0?

By "properly and safely" I mean that the pianist can use the proper technique without having to adjust or compensate in any way and can play without pain, strain, or risk of injury.

The first question is about making the piano accessible as an instrument to the entire population. The second question is also important because even those with large hands may still experience some pain or other challenges playing certain pieces of music. We'll see that the conventional piano keyboard is optimized to a hand size comprising less than 20% of the entire male population. For the other 80% of males and nearly 100% of females, the DS6.0 size (which David Steinbuhler refers to as the "Universal" size) is a more suitable maximum size, with even smaller sizes desirable for many players. Let's put some solid numbers on these claims.

HAND SPAN RESEARCH

The most recent and thorough large-scale survey of hand span variation among pianists was conducted by Rhonda Boyle, Robin Boyle, and Erica Booker in 2015. They investigated hand size, hand size variation by gender, age, and ethnicity, and the implications of these variations in piano performance. Their study analyzed hand span measurements from 473 adult pianists (student, amateur, and professional), supplemented with data from 216 non-pianist university students for general population comparison and 49 children and teenagers aged 9-17.[52]

---

[52] Boyle, R., Boyle, R., & Booker, E. (2015, July). "Pianist Hand Spans: Gender and Ethnic Differences and Implications for Piano Playing." In L. Edwards (Ed.), Proceedings of the 12th Australasian Piano Pedagogy Conference (p. 15-17). Australasian Piano Pedagogy Conference Association. https://appca.com.au/allproceedings/179%20PRPaper%20-%20Boyles-Booker.pdf.

They measured the maximum hand span from the tip of the thumb to the tip of the pinky when fully stretched. They also measured the span from index finger to pinky, as that helps provide a more complete picture of the size and stretching capability of the hand.[53]

Other variations in hand shape, such as having a small palm with longer fingers, or a large palm with shorter fingers, as well as variations in finger thickness, also influence piano playing ergonomics and technique. For example, longer fingers relative to palm size might provide an advantage in reaching the interior notes of chords. People with particularly thick fingers may have difficulty playing comfortably in between black keys on a conventional keyboard, which could be a disadvantage for those individuals even if their span is adequate.

It is also common for a person's right and left hands to have slightly different spans from thumb to pinky. This happens because the human body is naturally lateralized, meaning one side is often a bit different from the other. Usually, the difference in hand size or span is small and can depend on a person's sex and which hand they use more (i.e., their dominant hand). Studies show that the dominant hand often has a slightly larger span, but the difference is not usually very large and is not enough to affect the sizing of the keyboard chosen.[54]

These additional variations in hand shape will not be considered here, and the study authors call for more detailed future research on these nuanced aspects of hand shape and finger characteristics in relation to ergonomic keyboard design. Throughout this book, I refer only to the distance from thumb to pinky when discussing hand span, as this measurement is both the clearest and simplest to understand and also has the greatest impact on the performance capabilities of pianists.

The Results

The 2015 study found that there are significant gender and ethnic differences in hand span, with males generally having larger hands than females and some ethnic groups (e.g., Asians) tending to have smaller hand spans than Caucasians. The study also found that highly

---

[53] Ibid.
[54] Schwab, C. et al. (2025). "Enthesis Size and Hand Preference: Asymmetry in Humans and Nonhuman Primates." *Scientific Reports,* https://pmc.ncbi.nlm.nih.gov/articles/ PMC11922003/. Accessed August 24, 2025.

acclaimed solo performers often have larger hand spans, suggesting an advantage in playing the conventional piano keyboard.[55]

Specifically, male pianists had, on average, 1 inch greater spans between thumb and pinky than females. Nearly all individual males surpassed the average female hand span, with the top 83.7% of males' hand spans wider than the bottom 75% of females. There was also substantial variation among individuals of the same gender.[56]

Caucasian pianists generally had larger hand spans than Asian pianists. Among males, Caucasians' average thumb-to-pinky span was 0.3 inches larger than Asians'; for females, the difference was 0.2 inches. Gender differences persisted across ethnic groups: both Caucasian and Asian males had hand spans approximately one inch larger than females in their respective groups.[57]

Hand span also correlates with the level of achievement among pianists. Those recognized at the international level invariably have thumb-to-pinky spans exceeding 8.5 inches, with many surpassing 9.3 inches, and they are predominantly male. National-level performers typically exhibit intermediate hand sizes, while regional or amateur pianists display a broader range, including smaller hand spans. Notably, the disparity in hand size partly explains the gender imbalance among high-level performers, where men are disproportionately represented. However, due to limited data, no conclusive ethnic influence on performance acclaim could be established.[58]

Comparing pianists to the general population, the researchers found no major differences in average hand span among similarly aged groups, and pianists' slightly larger spans overall could be explained by the fact that people with small hands may be more likely to stop playing the piano early on because it feels physically difficult or uncomfortable, whereas those with larger hands often find it easier and more enjoyable, which can lead to greater success and motivation to continue.[59]

---

[55] Boyle, R., Boyle R., and Booker E., 10-24.
[56] Ibid., 10-12.
[57] Ibid., 13-19.
[58] Ibid., 19-24.
[59] Ibid., 25-34.

A small sample of children (49 in total) showed that hand span increases with age. Notably, the smallest adult female hand spans overlapped with those of many children, emphasizing the challenge for small-handed adults using the conventional keyboard.[60]

What are Small Hands, and How Many People Have Them?

The authors define "small hands" in the context of piano playing as those with a maximum thumb-to-pinky finger span under 8.5 inches, a threshold reached through an extensive evaluation that considers ergonomic, biomechanical, clinical, and performance factors. This definition emerges from an assessment of how hand size influences the physical challenges of playing on the conventional piano keyboard.[61]

In terms of practical piano performance, the authors analyzed how hand span correlates with the ability to play various intervals comfortably. They found that spans below 8.5 inches consistently result in discomfort and technical difficulty when playing octaves at speed and with ease, especially across the black keys, where the added reach and dexterity are more demanding. Moreover, statistical data from their survey reinforce this threshold: all internationally recognized pianists in the sample had hand spans exceeding 8.5 inches, indicating that falling below this measure represents a notable disadvantage for elite performance.[62]

Thus, converging evidence from biomechanics, clinical findings, piano pedagogy, and statistical analysis of accomplished performers supports 8.5 inches as a meaningful cutoff for defining "small hands" in piano playing. This benchmark reflects the ergonomic demands required to play a broad selection of standard repertoire comfortably and without physical strain on the conventional keyboard. The authors suggest this definition is practical and significant, marking the span below which pianists

---

[60] Ibid., 34-36.
[61] Ibid., 43-55.
[62] Ibid.

encounter increased technical, health, and performance challenges.[63]

The results strikingly reveal that the vast majority of female pianists have small hands based on this definition: approximately 87% of all adult female pianists fall below the 8.5-inch thumb-to-pinky threshold. In contrast, about 24% of adult male pianists are classified as having small hands. When ethnicity is factored in, disparities become even more pronounced. For example, about 30% of Asian male pianists and a staggering 94% of Asian female pianists have small hands, compared to roughly 20% of Caucasian males and 82% of Caucasian females within the same categories.[64]

The authors emphasize that these estimates are conservative, and the true prevalence of small hands among pianists globally may be even greater, particularly as the piano-playing population becomes increasingly diverse ethnically and includes large cohorts of Asian pianists. Furthermore, they suggest that even the 8.5-inch threshold for large hands–while the most reasonable threshold based on current evidence–may understate the extent of small-handedness among pianists. Many pianists with hand spans at or above this threshold still encounter ergonomic challenges and could benefit from narrower keyboards.[65]

The Zones

Boyle, Boyle, and Booker defined four distinct size categories based on the minimum hand stretch needed to play octaves, ninths, and tenths, plus a higher level for those who can play tenths comfortably. They designate these categories Zones A, B, C, and D.[66]

The table displayed in Figure 6.1 defines these zones by hand span and provides an indication of the intervals that can be reached by people in each zone.[67]

---

[63] Ibid.
[64] Ibid., 55-62.
[65] Ibid.
[66] Ibid., 55.
[67] Ibid., 53-56.

Zone	Thumb-to-Pinky Span	Category	Interval Possibilities
A	< 7.6 inches	Very small	Unable to play ninths even on the edge of the keys. Even octaves are difficult if possible at all.
B	7.6 inches → 8.5 inches	Small	Can play octaves mostly comfortably. Ninths are possible at full stretch. Most tenths unreachable. Some tenths may be reachable on the edge by people in the upper end of this zone.
C	8.5 inches → 9.4 inches	Large	Octaves are completely comfortable. Ninths are mostly comfortable. Can play tenths.
D	>= 9.4 inches	Very large	Can play tenths comfortably. Elevenths playable at least on the edge. Comfortable elevenths and twelfths on the edge may be possible for those at the upper end of this zone.

Figure 6.1 - The hand span zones.

People in Zones A and B have small or very small hands and cannot play the conventional keyboard fully and properly. People in Zone C have large hands, but they are not large enough to play everything with full comfort. People in Zone D have very large hands. These are the people for whom the conventional keyboard is properly sized. Note the threshold between Zones B and C–between small and large hands–is the 8.5-inch span defined previously.

The study presents the following graphical representation of the hand span data broken out into each zone.

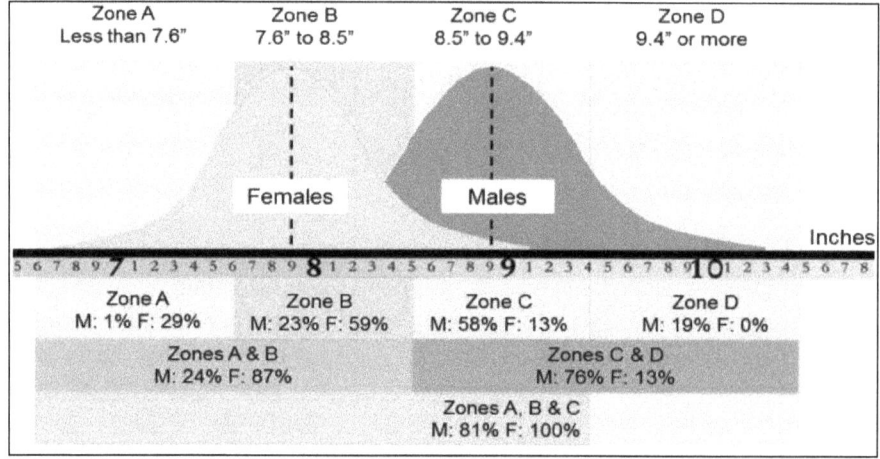

Figure 6.2 - Pianist thumb-to-pinky span broken into zones.[68]

IMPLICATIONS OF HAVING SMALL HANDS

Before analyzing the need for the more widespread use of narrower piano keyboards based on this data, it's important to review in more detail the physiologic effects of playing a conventional piano with small hands.

Pain and Injury Risk

A summary of research into physical risk factors affecting pianists highlights that hand size is a significant contributor to pain and injury in pianists. Studies in performing arts medicine have identified multiple contributors to piano-related discomfort, including technique, practice duration and intensity, posture, and genetic factors, but hand size consistently emerges as a key factor.

---

[68] Ibid., 57. Diagram reproduced with permission of the authors.

Women are disproportionately affected, with evidence indicating they experience pain or injury from playing the piano at rates up to 50% higher than men. In some studies, 70–80% of female pianists report pain or injury at some point in their playing careers.[69]

Clinical investigations have consistently shown that smaller hand span increases the risk of hand and forearm pain, especially when playing musical passages requiring wide stretches, such as octaves and large chords. These motions can force the thumb and pinky finger into extreme positions, potentially leading to overuse injuries like de Quervain tendinopathy, tenosynovitis, and lateral elbow tendinopathy.[70]

Recent epidemiological studies confirm that hand size and related factors like finger span, hand strength, and speed have a statistically significant relationship with pain and playing-related musculoskeletal disorders. Upper limb disorders are strongly correlated with reduced hand span. Research also shows that children and young musicians suffer similar types and rates of injury as adults, underlining that vulnerability exists across all age groups.[71]

Other Consequences of Having Small Hands

Pianists with smaller hand spans often work at the extremes of the physiological limits of their hand muscles and joints when attempting to play the conventional keyboard, which can significantly increase muscular tension, fatigue, and reduce fine motor control. These physical barriers can impact the choice of repertoire for pianists.[72]

In terms of repertoire, the most common sources of strain were passages requiring octaves or large chords, which consistently caused physical stress for those with smaller hands. It's not even

---

[69] "Epidemiological and Clinical Studies." *Pianists for Alternatively Sized Keyboards,* https://paskpiano.org/epidemiological-and-clinical-studies/. Accessed July 15, 2025.
[70] Ibid.
[71] Ibid.
[72] Boyle, R., Boyle R., and Booker E., pp. 43-55.

possible for these pianists to play much of the classical music from the Romantic period and early 20th century, particularly works by Rachmaninoff, Brahms, and other composers with large chords throughout their compositions. Reflecting these challenges, Boyle, Boyle, and Booker found that all 12 of the elite soloists they surveyed had hand spans greater than 8.5 inches, highlighting the significant barriers small-handed pianists may face in reaching the highest levels of performance.[73]

Indeed, given that the average woman's hand span is one inch less than the average man's, if hand span negatively affects a player's success in elite competitions, we would expect to see differences in competition outcomes between men and women. Rhonda Boyle has compiled data on the ratio of female to male prize winners dating back to the 1960s. Her results, shown in Figure 6.3, reveal a consistent and significant disparity in competition results favoring men that has persisted for decades.[74]

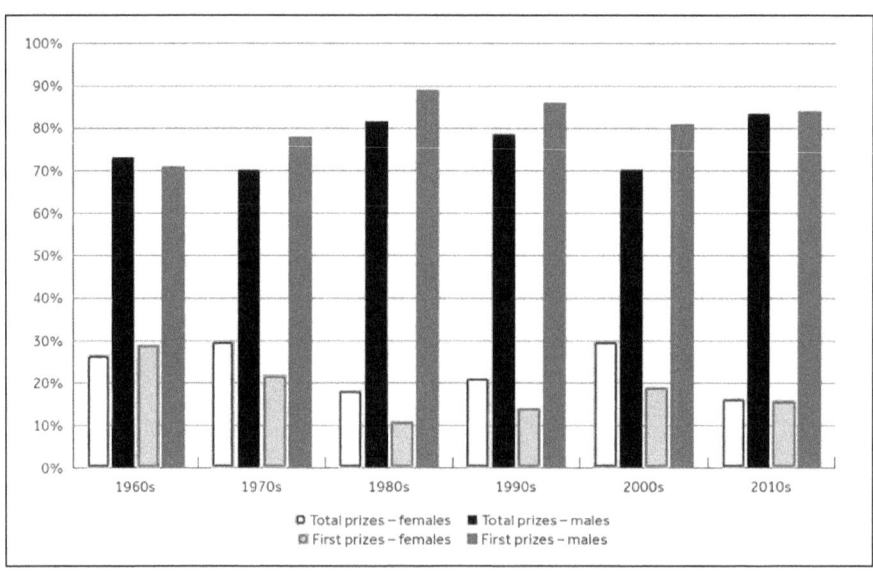

Figure 6.3 - Proportion of female prize winners by decade across 13 major piano competitions.[75]

---

[73] Ibid.
[74] Boyle, Rhonda. "The Real Reason Men Dominate Major Piano Competitions." *International Piano*, Autumn 2024.
[75] Ibid. Diagram reproduced with permission of the author.

While it is easy to point to potential bias among juries or ingrained conservatory sexism as the root of these gender disparities, statistical and historical analyses suggest the effect of jury discrimination is negligible compared to physical barriers. For example, women do as well as or better than men in youth competitions, but their representation drops steeply in older age groups and in the transition to professional-level repertoire–exactly when hand span requirements become critical. Even when reviewing detailed voting patterns in major competitions such as the International Fryderyk Chopin Piano Competition, no bias against women was detected. Further, in competitions that focus on the music of Bach and Mozart, the disparity between men and women disappears. What's different about Bach and Mozart? Smaller chords, easily playable by smaller hands.[76]

In summary, the research has found that not only do small-handed pianists consistently experience more pain when playing and face a higher risk of injury, they are limited in the repertoire they can play, and they also face a severe disadvantage in competition, seldom able to compete successfully at the highest level. This is a sad situation for those of us who love music, love playing the piano, and want to play the music we choose without physical limitations.

Bottom-Line Analysis

Let's get to the bottom line and answer the two questions posed at the beginning of this chapter:

■ How many people require a narrower keyboard in order to play a full repertoire of piano music properly and safely?

■ How many people who have hands that are large enough to accommodate the conventional keyboard would nonetheless benefit from having a smaller keyboard, such as the DS6.0?

[76] Ibid.

We'll use the hand span research results from Boyle, Boyle, and Booker, reproduced in Figure 6.4, to answer these two questions.

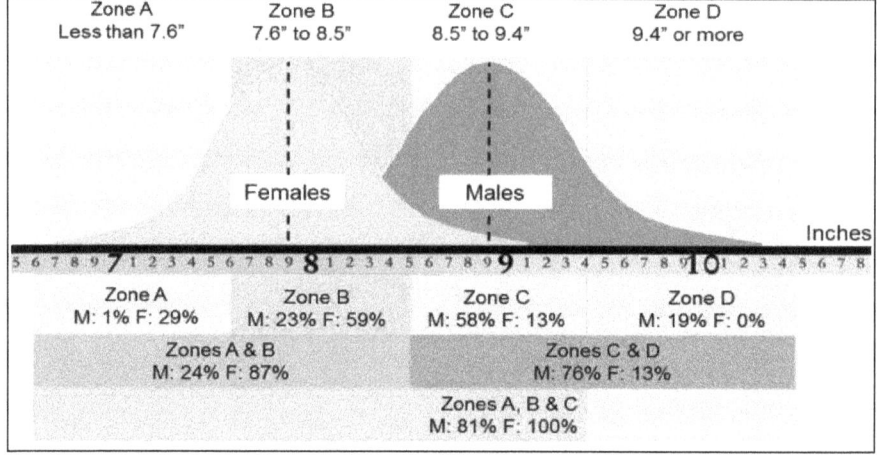

Figure 6.4 - Pianist thumb-to-pinky span broken into zones.[77]

Here is the breakdown of the needs and capabilities of people in each of the four hand span zones:

- Those in Zone A absolutely need a narrower keyboard.

- Those in Zone B need a narrower keyboard to play comfortably and safely in the majority of cases.

- Those in Zone C do not need a narrower keyboard to play in most cases, but to avoid some discomfort, eliminate the risk of injury, and enable them to play everything without any physical restrictions at all, they would benefit from a narrower keyboard.

- Those in Zone D do not need a narrower keyboard and would derive very little, if any, benefit from it.

I will group Zones A and B together as the population that needs a narrower keyboard. Zone C (together with A and B) would benefit from a narrower keyboard. Only Zone D does not need or derive any benefit from a narrower keyboard.

---

[77] Boyle, R., Boyle R., and Booker E., 57. Diagram reproduced with permission of the authors.

So let's take the numbers presented in the diagram in Figure 6.4. For men:

- 19% of men have hands that are sized properly (Zone D)

- 24% of men have hands that are too small and require DS5.5 (Zones A and B)

- The remaining 57% have hands that can deal with DS6.5 but would benefit from DS6.0 (Zone C)

For women:

- 0% of women have hands that are sized properly (Zone D)

- 87% of women have hands that are too small and require DS5.5 (Zones A and B)

- The remaining 13% have hands that can deal with DS6.5 but would benefit from DS6.0 (Zone C)

Assuming the population is evenly split among men and women, this means that:

- 55.5% of the overall population have hands that are too small and require DS5.5

- 35% of the overall population have hands that can deal with DS6.5 but would benefit from DS6.0

- 9.5% of the overall population have hands that are sized properly

- 90.5% of the overall population would benefit from having DS6.0/5.5 available

We're only considering the adult population here. When you factor in children, the numbers will be even more heavily skewed towards the need for narrower keyboards. Essentially no child other than some teenage boys (less than 19% of them based on the adult male number) has hands that are large enough to play the conventional DS6.5 keyboard properly and safely.

Conclusion

Based on the most recent and thorough hand span data available, the answers to the two questions posed above are:

■ *More than half of the adult population, 55.5%, has hands that are too small to play the conventional DS6.5 keyboard fully and safely.*

■ *And an overwhelming majority, 90.5%, of adults would benefit from having at least the DS6.0 keyboard available to them.*

So it's not just me! Countless pianists share the need for a narrower keyboard, even though very few of them may realize it.

Chapter 7

THE NAYSAYERS

Responding To Opposition

Despite the obvious benefits of narrower keyboards for a large number of pianists in need of them, it has taken more than three decades for the idea to gain meaningful traction. Only recently have a few acoustic piano manufacturers like Hailun, August Förster, and Steingraeber & Söhne started offering narrower keyboards as optional features on select models. Similarly, digital pianos with narrower key widths are just beginning to appear on the market.

Why has it taken so long for this concept to gain acceptance? Without some kind of catalyst or major shift in thinking, it may still be years before variable keyboard sizes become mainstream. Even then, it could take many more years before society views the past norm as unfair and exclusionary.

In this chapter we will explore some of the objections and concerns that some raise about narrower keyboards, many of which have contributed to the slow acceptance of this important innovation.

LACK OF AVAILABILITY AND STANDARDIZATION

The Concerns

Large manufacturers have been reluctant to mass-produce narrower keyboards, often viewing the market as too niche or commercially uncertain to justify the investment. As a result, options for alternative sizes remain limited, and there is little industry-wide standardization. The lack of standardized key sizes could lead to confusion and compatibility issues for pianists–especially those who practice or perform on multiple instruments–since they would not be able to rely on each piano having the same key dimensions.

The Response

It seems we may be facing a classic chicken-and-egg dilemma in the piano market. While the current demand for narrower keyboards appears limited, this lack of demand could be largely due to the fact that such options have historically been unavailable or offered only in limited supply. If manufacturers do not produce and promote narrower keyboard models, potential buyers simply won't have the opportunity to choose them. Consequently, this restricts market growth and perpetuates the perception that the demand is too small to justify expanding the product range.

Ultimately, the future growth of alternative keyboard sizes depends on manufacturers' willingness to innovate and take a chance on these products, potentially complemented by growing consumer demand fueled by increased awareness. Hailun, August Förster, and Steingraeber & Söhne have started this process. Unfortunately, there remain a number of other objections and concerns to wide adoption of narrower keyboard alternatives. Time will tell if demand increases.

Regarding standardization, as discussed in Chapter 5, the DS Standard Foundation has developed three main standard adult keyboard sizes (DS6.5, DS6.0®, and DS5.5®), plus options for children. Their research and multiple university studies show these sizes meet the needs of nearly all adult hands, and standardized labeling using the trademarked DS nomenclature encourages wider adoption by manufacturers. These standards offer pianists the confidence of knowing exactly what to expect when they arrive at a venue. They would know what to request and would be able to trust that it would be provided.[78]

COST AND PRACTICAL LIMITATIONS

The Concerns

Custom keyboards are often more expensive and can require long wait times. The high cost stems from limited production and the ability to retrofit only a small number of pianos per year.

The Response

As narrower keyboards of standard sizes become more widely adopted and demand begins to grow, economies of scale can come into play. Mass production of these standardized sizes should significantly lower manufacturing costs over time, making them more affordable and accessible to a broader range of consumers, including students, schools, music venues, and professional pianists.

To streamline this process and better serve the needs of piano buyers, manufacturers could offer consumers a choice of keyboard sizes at the point of purchase, just as many other instruments and consumer products come in various sizes or configurations. This choice could be as simple as selecting between the DS sizes (including the conventional DS6.5) when ordering a digital piano, acoustic grand, or upright.[79] Again, several acoustic piano manufacturers have started offering this option. If more piano manufacturers would follow their lead, the opportunities for pianists would be expanded, and the costs would decrease.

---

[78] Steinbuhler, David. "The DS Standard®." *Standard Foundation,* https://dsstandardfoundation.org/the-standards/. Accessed July 17, 2025.
[79] "How Many Sizes?" *Pianists for Alternatively Sized Keyboards,* https://paskpiano.org/how-many-sizes/. Accessed July 18, 2025.

Offering size options at the outset reduces logistical complexity for pianists and institutions in several important ways:

- Pianists would no longer need to retrofit or customize their instruments after purchase, saving both time and money.

- Music schools, universities, and teaching studios could standardize their inventory by providing each of the available sizes, offering students a more comfortable and ergonomic fit from the beginning.

- For performance venues and piano rental companies, having clearly labeled keyboard size options would simplify planning for recitals and performances by matching pianists with instruments suited to their physical needs.

By shifting some of the customization process upstream, directly into the hands of manufacturers at the time of production, the entire ecosystem becomes more responsive and efficient. Over time, this could help redefine what is considered "standard," emphasizing adaptability and accessibility over a rigid uniformity that does not serve all users equally.

Tradition and Cultural Resistance

The Concerns

The piano world is resistant to change, valuing tradition over innovation. Some musicians see adapting to the "standard" as a badge of honor, and narrower alternative keyboards may be perceived as "cheating" or an admission of weakness, risking career advancement.[80]

---

[80] "Overcoming the Barriers." *Pianists for Alternatively Sized Keyboards,* https://paskpiano. org/overcoming-the-barriers/. Accessed July 18, 2025.

The Response

Resisting change solely in the name of tradition overlooks the broader goal of music: enabling expressive, artistic performance at the highest level by as many people as possible. While the piano world has long prized tradition, history also shows that meaningful innovation has often met initial resistance only to become accepted, even embraced, over time.

Indeed, some musicians may view mastery of the conventional keyboard as a badge of honor and fear that narrower alternatives could be seen as shortcuts or signs of weakness. However, this perspective limits the potential of the instrument and the people who play it. Hand size, like vocal range or body type in other instruments, is not an indicator of talent or work ethic–it's a physical reality. In most instruments, accommodations for physical differences are standard practice. Trumpets come in various bore sizes; violins come in half and quarter sizes; woodwind instruments offer key extensions for smaller hands. Should we expect a child to play a full-sized cello immediately, and judge him–or even a small adult–for using a ¾ size? Of course not.

Providing narrower keyboard options isn't about lowering standards–it's about removing artificial barriers. A standardized octave size was never meant to be a test of character or determination; it was a practical design choice that reflected the needs and preferences of the time, and it suited the large European male pianists who wanted a bigger sound from the instrument. The conventional keyboard fit their hands well and supported the musical demands of their era.

As we've seen, most pianists don't have very large hands (in Zone D) like the 19th century virtuosic concert pianists. Most pianists have more average or smaller sized hands. Having access to appropriately sized keyboards enables better technique development, greater ease of musical expression, and injury prevention, allowing all pianists to reach their full potential.

It's worth noting that acceptance of narrower keyboard alternative sizes is growing within professional and educational circles, not as a way to "make things easier," but to make them more fair. Professional competitions, universities, and conservatories are beginning to recognize that elite performance and physical accessibility can and should coexist.

Ultimately, valuing musical artistry over physical conformity is not "cheating"; it's progress. Just as the piano evolved from the harpsichord, and digital technologies opened new creative possibilities, embracing alternative keyboard sizes honors the spirit of innovation that has always shaped music history.

ADAPTATION AND PORTABILITY ISSUES

The Concerns

Some pianists worry about the difficulty of switching between conventional and alternative key sizes, especially for performances or competitions at different venues. This concern extends to sight-reading, muscle memory, and technical reliability.

The Response

Dr. Carol Leone of Southern Methodist University conducted the first-ever study on narrow keyboards, and SMU was the first university worldwide to integrate narrow keyboards into its performance curriculum. Dr. Leone reports that students who switch between standard and narrower keyboards adapt remarkably quickly, often within just two weeks. Her ergonomic studies confirm that muscle memory and technique transfer effectively with training, and she advocates for making multiple key widths available for both education and performance.[81]

In fact, I believe the two week benchmark may only refer to the time it takes to feel 100% proficient with the narrower keyboard for the first time, because Dr. Leone has also reported that pianists find it easy to adapt to these keyboards, typically needing less than an hour of practice to become comfortable. She and her students are able to

---

[81] Leone, Carol. "A New "Key" to Success: Addressing Pianists' Injuries Through Keyboard Size." *Clavier Companion*, May/June 2014.

switch smoothly between all three types of keyboards (DS6.5, DS6.0, and DS5.5), even during the same performance. In 2014, over the course of four days, Dr. Leone successfully recorded a recital CD using a Steinway D fitted with each of its three keyboards (DS6.5, DS6.0, and DS5.5). This versatility allowed her to perform a wide range of repertoire, including challenging pieces she would usually avoid, such as Chopin's Ballade in G Minor.[82]

My experience with all three keyboard sizes, as well as the DS5.1, has been comparable. In the next chapter, I'll share the story of my visit to David Steinbuhler and what it was like to play on all four sizes in one sitting. For now, I can report that the transition to the DS6.0 required no adjustment whatsoever. I was immediately able to play it without any conscious adjustment. Adapting to the DS5.5 took about 20–30 minutes, while the DS5.1 required a bit more time. When I first tried the DS5.1 at Steinbuhler's residence, I didn't fully acclimate to it, but it has since become the size I use most often. It ultimately took a couple of weeks to become completely proficient on this much narrower keyboard.

So the extensive evidence gathered by Dr. Carol Leone, myself, and many others who regularly play on narrower keyboards clearly shows that adjusting to different pianos at various venues–including those with conventional and alternative key widths–is simply not a problem. Pianists report that after acclimating to multiple keyboard sizes, they can move between instruments with ease, regardless of the venue or keyboard configuration. This adaptability holds true not just in practice studios, but also in high-pressure settings such as performances and recordings. The collective experience of those using differently sized keyboards strongly suggests that concerns about adjustment barriers are largely unfounded, reinforcing the practical viability of offering pianists more choice in keyboard size.

I would also argue that the majority of pianists practice and play primarily, and often exclusively, at home on their own instrument. Many pianists rarely if ever play outside the home. Small venues such as community centers, coffee houses, or similar small event spaces

---

[82] Leone, Carol. "Size is Key." *Clavier Companion, Frances Clark Center for Keyboard Pedagogy*, vol. 7, no. 5, September/October 2015.

often lack an acoustic piano, and such venues rely on the performer bringing their own digital piano or keyboard.

For the rare musician who does perform regularly in concert halls or theaters, it is true that they must use whatever instrument the venue provides. Still, as previously discussed, this issue can be addressed by keeping alternative keyboards available. Given the major investment concert halls make in high-value instruments like a nine-foot Steinway D, it does not seem unreasonable to expect that they could stock one or two narrower keyboards that can be swapped out at the artist's request.

MUSICAL AND TECHNICAL CONCERNS

The Concerns

There are fears that narrower keys might alter the tone, restrict expressive power, or hinder advanced technical achievement. Skeptics worry about loss of authenticity, instrument durability, or unforeseen ergonomic issues.

The Response

It is true that replacing the entire action of a piano will alter its sound. The hammers are part of the action, and they are the components that strike the strings and create the sound. As we saw in Chapter 5, however, David Steinbuhler conducted extensive research into piano actions and key design to ensure that the feel and expressive power of the keyboard would remain unchanged. One of his designs for keyboard retrofits keeps the original hammers and wippens and places the rest of the action stack on a new frame with the new keyboard. In this scenario, the sound of the piano will be unchanged since the hammers are unchanged.

If a piano is originally designed with the narrower keyboard rather than it being swapped out later as a retrofit, then this concern is completely moot. The piano would have exactly the tone and feel that the manufacturer intended. If multiple keyboard sizes for a single piano were needed and they were all made by the original piano manufacturer, then again the pianist would be assured that the piano has the tone and feel the manufacturer intended.

This is not just theoretical. Actual use and preliminary ergonomic studies at Université de Montréal, as well as previously published research, show that narrower actions maintain all expressive and sonic potential; for small-handed pianists, they actually allow for better accuracy and greater dynamic and tonal control across the full repertoire. For large-handed pianists, however, standard widths remain preferable, reinforcing the value of choice.[83]

Conclusion

It is difficult to get people to change their paradigm of thinking. Those fortunate enough to have large hands may understandably struggle to grasp the disadvantages many pianists face on a conventional keyboard. For them, it can be hard to imagine the physical obstacles or discomfort others encounter.

Meanwhile, some of those who would most benefit from narrower keyboards may not fully understand the extent of those benefits for themselves. Many have simply accepted the conventional keyboard as an unchangeable feature of the instrument, believing any physical strain or limitation is just something to endure. In some cases, players may never have even thought to themselves that they've had more difficulty, challenges, or pain than other people have; and even if they do realize it, they may take pride in overcoming their challenges or enduring discomfort as part of their personal journey with the piano.

Many people may question why we can't simply adapt in various ways. Can't play tenths? Just roll them. Can't play certain pieces without pain? Exclude those pieces from your repertoire. It takes more effort and time for you to learn certain pieces because of the physical challenges imposed by the large keyboard size? Good for you–you've done a great job mastering the instrument!

---

[83] "A Piano for Smaller Hands Comes to UdeM." *UdeMNouvelles*, https://nouvelles. umontreal.ca/en/article/2024/04/30/a-piano-for-smaller-hands-comes-to-udem/. Accessed July 18, 2025.

These suggestions aren't about achieving greater musical expression; they are simply about accepting and adapting to the instrument as it currently exists. Rolling tenths creates a different sound from being able to play them as a chord. Choosing repertoire based on hand size is limiting and ultimately discouraging to someone who wants to master the instrument, the music, and their artistry, or who simply wants to play the music they most enjoy. Spending time struggling with physical challenges pianists with larger hands typically don't have to face is a waste of time that could be better spent learning new pieces or developing greater expressiveness at the piano.

And this is why we need narrower keyboard alternatives. Let's define a piano and break down the definition. A piano is a musical instrument. Music has been described by many authors and philosophers, including English author Arnold Bennett, as the language of the soul.[84] An instrument is a mechanism that extends the capabilities of your body and enables you to perform some task or accomplish some goal. So as a musical instrument, a piano can be thought of as a mechanism–or an extension of the body–that allows the soul to express itself. If my soul wants to express itself in a certain way, the instrument is not serving its purpose if it hinders or even prevents me from making that musical expression.

Despite any objections to the contrary, we need narrower keyboards for a very simple reason: to allow every person who plays the piano to have the ability to utilize the full breadth of musical expression this instrument was meant to provide.

---

[84] Bennett, Arnold. *Sacred and Profane Love.* Project Gutenberg, 2004. https://www. gutenberg.org/files/11360/11360-h/11360-h.htm. Accessed July 18, 2025.

Chapter 8

A MATTER OF SIZE

How Narrower Keyboards Give
Players Bigger Hands

Let's explore how the narrower DS Standard® keyboard sizes overcome differences in hand span among pianists of all proportions. In Chapter 6 we explored the available hand span data and saw that hand spans can be classified into four zones of increasing size, A through D. Zones A and B are the small hand zones, and Zones C and D are the large hand zones. The dividing mark that separates small from large hands is a span of 8.5 inches from thumb to pinky.

The DS Standard sizes are designed so that all players can effectively be in Zone C at a minimum. That means that all players can effectively have large hands when playing the piano. The conventional piano keyboard is optimized for those in Zone D, however. As we saw, 90% of the overall population is outside of Zone D, and therefore even those in Zone C can benefit from a narrower keyboard.

Let's use hand and keyboard diagrams to illustrate how the various DS Standard sizes benefit players in each zone. For each zone, we'll look at the average hand span on the conventional DS6.5

keyboard, then compare it to the keyboard size that advances that player at least to Zone C. This approach will clearly demonstrate the ergonomic advantages provided by appropriately-sized keyboards.

The data in Boyle, Boyle, and Booker's study[85] does not break out hand spans in a way that allows a determination of the average hand span among all players within a specific zone. However, we can estimate what those averages might be based on the hand span data chart we evaluated in Chapter 6, reproduced in Figure 8.1.

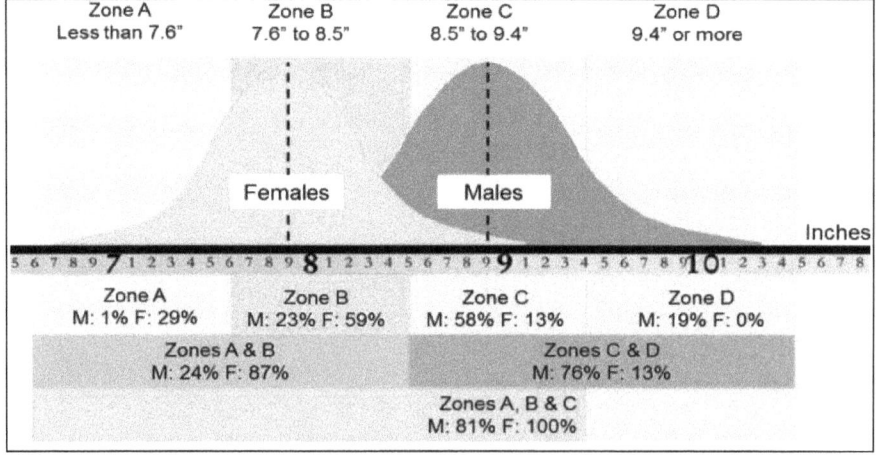

Figure 8.1 - Pianist thumb-to-pinky span broken into zones.[86]

I propose the following estimates for the average hand span among all people (men and women together) who are within each zone:

- Zone A - 7.4 inches

- Zone B - 8.0 inches

- Zone C - 8.8 inches

- Zone D - 9.6 inches

[85] Boyle, R., Boyle, R., & Booker, E. (2015, July). "Pianist Hand Spans: Gender and Ethnic Differences and Implications for Piano Playing." In L. Edwards (Ed.), *Proceedings of the 12th Australasian Piano Pedagogy Conference.* Australasian Piano Pedagogy Conference Association. https://appca.com.au/allproceedings/179%20PRPaper%20-%20Boyles-Booker.pdf.
[86] Ibid., 57. Diagram reproduced with permission of the authors.

Even if these estimates are off by 1- or 2-tenths of an inch, they still represent reasonable averages that are each well within their respective zones.

Average Zone C Player

We'll start with Zone C players. These are the players who already have large hands, but they can still benefit from moving into Zone D. Using the values above as the average hand span for each zone, Figure 8.2 illustrates what the average Zone C player's hands look like on the conventional DS6.5 keyboard.

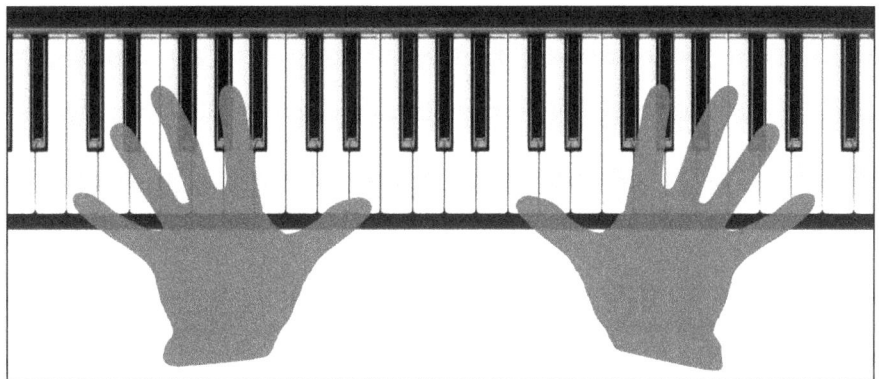

Figure 8.2 - Average Zone C hands on conventional DS6.5 keyboard.

When looking at these diagrams, remember that they represent the full stretch of the hands. For example, the Zone C player's hands are open to 8.8 inches, the average maximum span among all Zone C players. They cannot be stretched open any further.

As discussed previously and as can be seen in this diagram, Zone C players can play ninths with no difficulty. The tenths are reachable, but since we're looking at a white to white tenth in this diagram (a relatively small tenth), it is clear that some of the larger tenths must be played on the edge of the keys with maximum stretch, and some of the tenths may be out of reach.

Let's now move the average Zone C player to the DS6.0 keyboard. This is what the average Zone C player's hands look like on a DS6.0 keyboard:

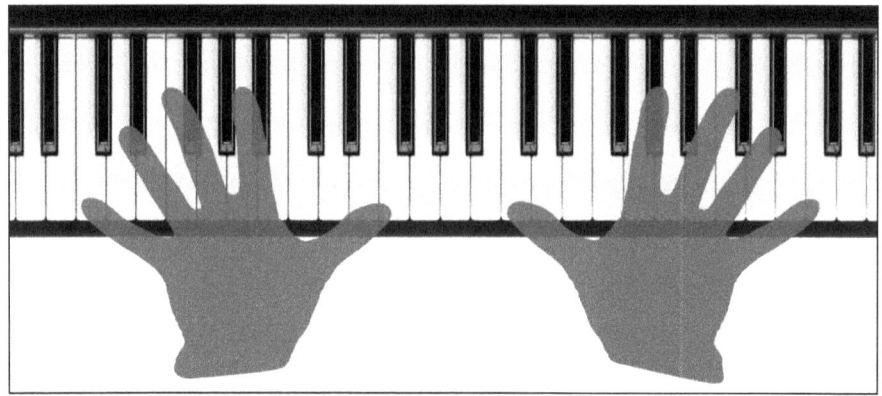

Figure 8.3 - Average Zone C hands on DS6.0 keyboard.

Now the Zone C player is able to just touch the elevenths. They are most likely not playable for the average Zone C player on DS6.0, but that extra reach brings all of the tenth intervals into reach. Many of them are comfortable, and all of them are reachable. The Zone C player is now very similar to a Zone D player (someone with very large hands) on the conventional keyboard.

Average Zone B Player

This is what the average Zone B player's hands look like on a conventional DS6.5 keyboard:

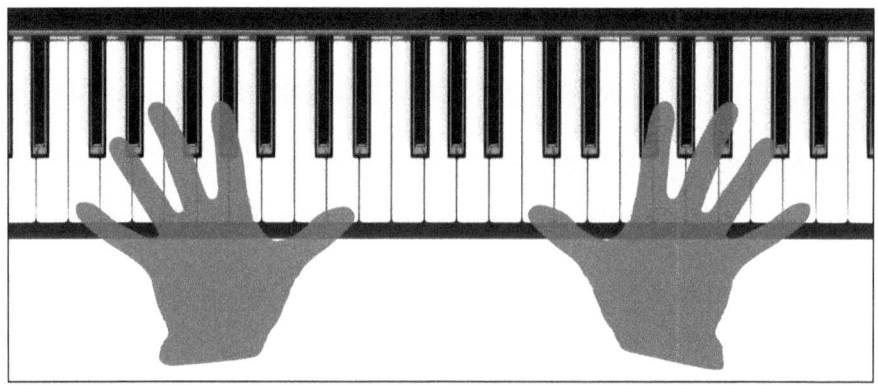

Figure 8.4 - Average Zone B hands on conventional DS6.5 keyboard.

For the Zone B player, the octaves are comfortable and many of the ninths can be played at full stretch on the edges of the keys.

Let's now move the average Zone B player to the DS5.5 keyboard. This is what the average Zone B player's hands look like on a DS5.5 keyboard:

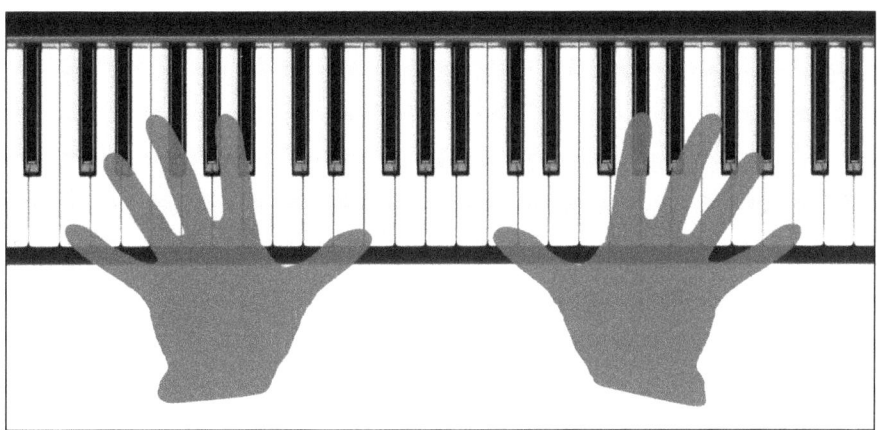

Figure 8.5 - Average Zone B hands on DS5.5 keyboard.

Now the Zone B player can reach all the ninths comfortably, and most of the tenths are playable, although they will require the full stretch of the player's hands. The Zone B player is now very similar to a Zone C player (someone with large hands) on the conventional keyboard.

Average Zone A Player

Finally, Figure 8.6 on the next page shows what the average Zone A player's hands look like on the conventional DS6.5 keyboard.

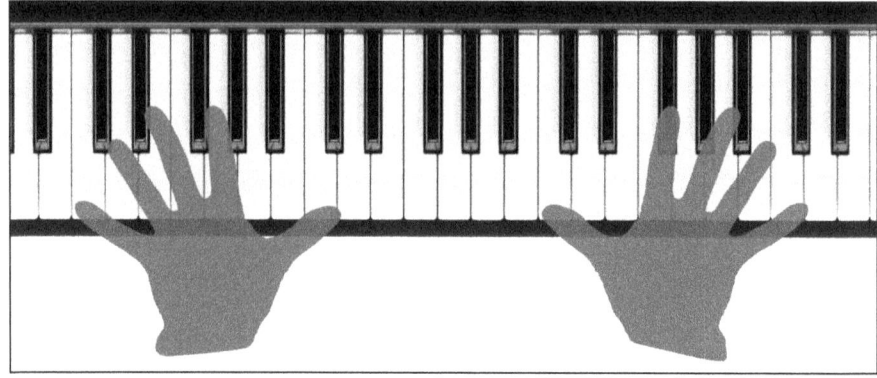

Figure 8.6 - Average Zone A hands on conventional DS6.5 keyboard.

This player can just play an octave. The ninths are completely out of reach, even on the edge of the keys.

Let's first move the average Zone A player to the DS5.5 keyboard. This is what the average Zone A player's hands look like on a DS5.5 keyboard:

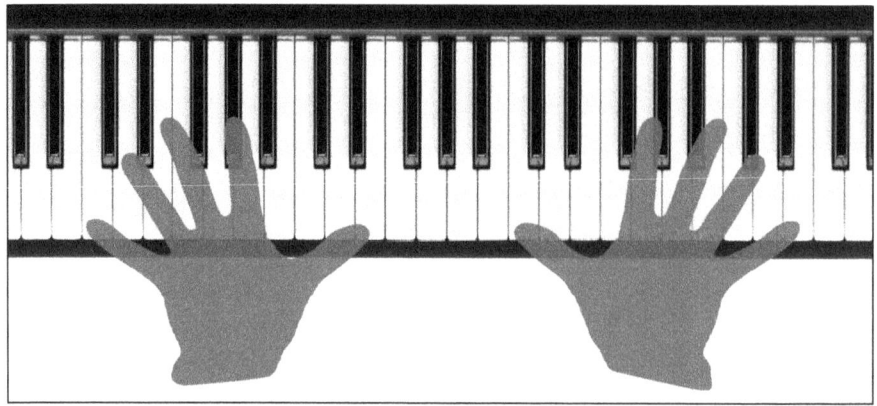

Figure 8.7 - Average Zone A hands on DS5.5 keyboard.

The ninths are now playable. Some of them will be comfortable, and some will need to be played with full stretch on the edge of the keys. It appears from the diagram that some of the tenths may be reachable, but there may not be quite enough extension into the tenth to make it playable without sounding the adjacent key.

Now let's move the Zone A player to the DS5.1 keyboard. This is what the average Zone A player's hands look like on a DS5.1 keyboard:

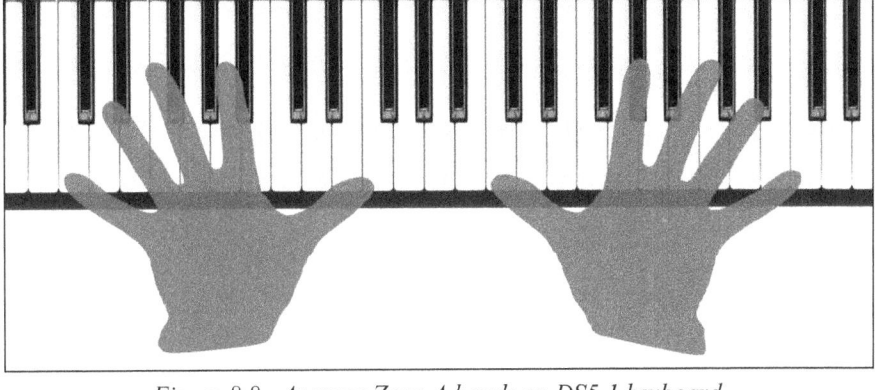

Figure 8.8 - Average Zone A hands on DS5.1 keyboard.

Now the Zone A player can reach all the ninths comfortably and most, if not all of the tenths are playable, although the larger tenths will require the full stretch of the player's hands. The Zone A player is now very similar to a Zone C player (someone with large hands) on the conventional keyboard.

Conclusion

From all of these diagrams, it is clear that shifting to the next smaller DS Standard size advances the player with the average hand size in their zone into the next larger zone. With the DS Standard sizes, nearly all players can effectively have large hands on the piano keyboard.

With an understanding of the benefits of narrower keyboards and how to choose the right size, it's time to return to my journey to find my own custom keyboard.

Chapter 9

FINDING MY FIT

*Determining the Keyboard Size
that Fits Best*

Until recently, I kept a 6'7" Bösendorfer grand piano in my home. Bösendorfer is the piano Oscar Peterson preferred–he played the 9-foot Imperial concert grand–and I had become enamored with its distinctive sound. In the early 2000s, I first discovered the possibility of retrofitting my instrument with a narrower keyboard from David Steinbuhler. Ultimately, I chose not to pursue this modification–partly, I admit, for some of the naysayers' reasons described earlier. My primary concern wasn't so much about losing the ability to switch back to a conventional keyboard in terms of technical capability, but rather that my repertoire would become limited when returning to a conventional-size instrument. I worried that while I might develop a broader repertoire and a more sophisticated approach on the narrower keyboard, I'd lose access to some of that progress when playing on a conventional keyboard.

Looking back, I realize these concerns were only partially justified. Since I rarely perform outside my home, the issue of switching between keyboard sizes is largely irrelevant. Of course, a significant reason I haven't performed publicly as much is that I haven't developed my piano skills and repertoire to the level I aspire to, which, if achieved, would motivate me to perform more often. Over time, I found myself increasingly drawn to digital instruments. This shift made sense: with a digital piano, I could bring my own instrument wherever I needed to play, ensuring I never had to sacrifice technique or repertoire regardless of the setting.

Narrow Keys NK 5.5 Digital Keyboard

In 2022 I discovered the Narrow Keys website and learned that they were preparing to begin manufacturing a professional-level instrument with a DS5.5 keyboard. I was interested at once and eagerly awaited their announcement. Only a few weeks after joining their mailing list, I received an email saying they were starting production on the first 10 instruments. Each instrument was to be made individually–a slow, manual process. After the first 10 instruments were built and shipped, Narrow Keys intended to make more, but it wasn't clear what their timeline would be. I wanted to make sure I was able to get one of the first 10 instruments, so I joined the waiting list as quickly as possible. To my extreme disappointment I learned that I was #11 in line. But a month or so later, I received an exciting email from Narrow Keys. Another customer asked to be moved to the bottom of the waiting list, making me #10!

Then the wait began. As the weeks passed, I became more and more anxious about the new keyboard, and I was growing impatient with the wait, which turned out to be much longer than I anticipated. I stumbled across a small 61-key Korg MIDI keyboard with a 5.5-

inch octave. It was inexpensive, so I bought it just to see what it would be like.

It was a cheap keyboard–it offered very little control and really did not feel that great to play. It wasn't meant to be played as a digital keyboard. Rather it was intended as a MIDI input device to be used by composers and arrangers. The keys were not only narrower but also much shorter than in a conventional keyboard, which made it really difficult to play some pieces. However, it did give me a feel for what the NK 5.5 with its DS5.5 keyboard would be like–it would be a big step in the right direction.

DS5.5: STILL TOO BIG?

As I experimented with the 5.5-inch octave Korg keyboard, I soon discovered that I still faced limitations. Once my NK 5.5 arrived, I was able to confirm what I had learned, and I discovered what I was able to play and what still posed challenges for me.

Let's take a look at some of the chords and voicings I introduced in Chapter 4 to get an idea of what was now possible and what was still out of reach for me on a DS5.5 keyboard.

Left Hand Voicings

We'll start with some left hand voicings. For simplicity, let's consider only seventh chords voiced as root-seventh-third. These are the most common larger voicings I need to play in the left hand. Here is a representative sample of the seventh chords I can reach on the DS5.5.

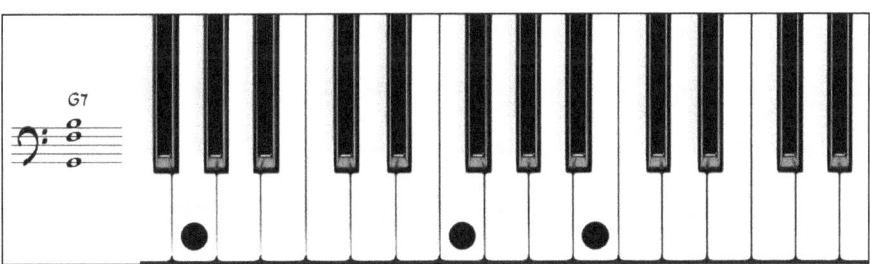

Figure 9.1 - Example of a G7 chord I can play on a DS5.5 keyboard.

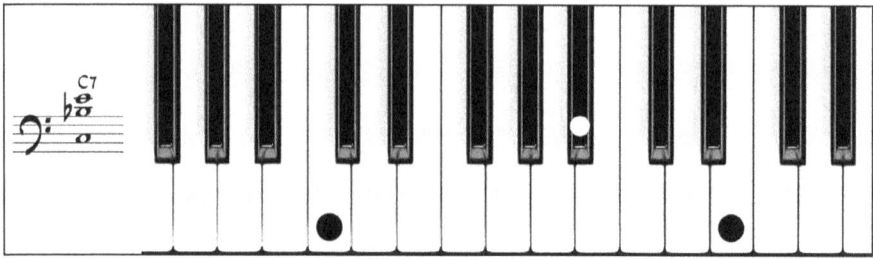

Figure 9.2 - Example of a C7 chord I can play on a DS5.5 keyboard.

But here are examples of chords that are still just out of reach for me on a DS5.5 keyboard:

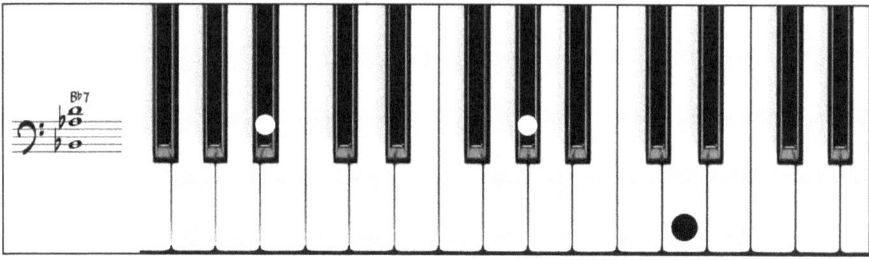

Figure 9.3 - Example of a B♭7 chord I still can't reach on a DS5.5 keyboard.

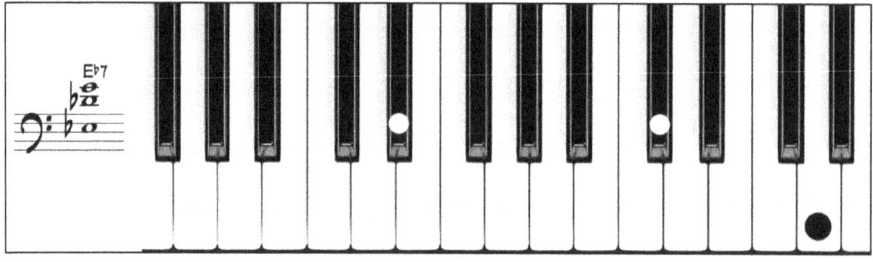

Figure 9.4 - Example of an E♭7 chord I still can't reach on a DS5.5 keyboard.

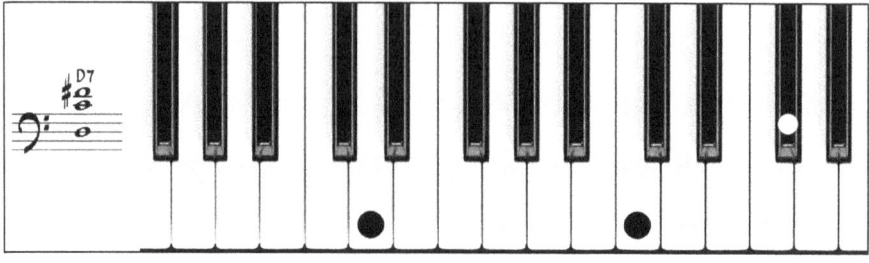

Figure 9.5 - Example of a D7 chord I still can't reach on a DS5.5 keyboard.

In some cases if I drop the middle note, I can play just the tenth interval. For example, I can't play the full D7 voicing in Figure 9.5, but I can play this:

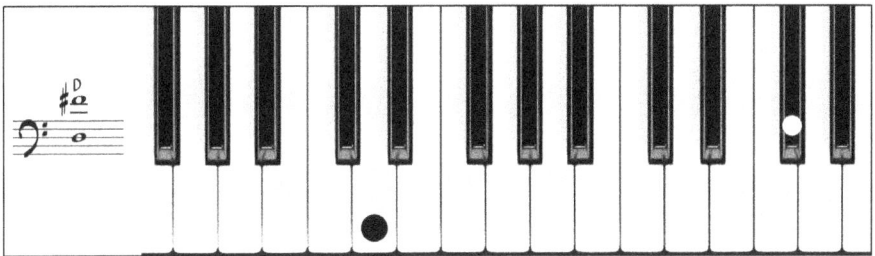

Figure 9.6 - Major tenth interval (in D) with no intermediate note.

There are even larger tenth spans that are of course out of reach as well. For example:

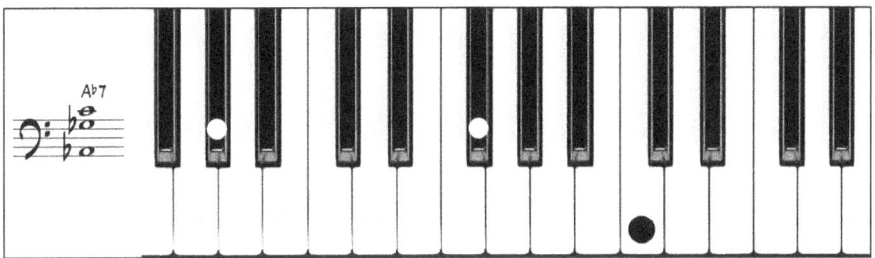

Figure 9.7 - Very wide A♭7 chord, unreachable by me on a DS5.5 keyboard.

Right Hand Voicings

In the right hand, I am able to play most simple tenths on the DS5.5 keyboard. The span of my right hand is actually smaller than my left hand by about 0.1-0.2 inches, so there are some differences in my reach with each hand. Black to black tenths are playable with my right hand:

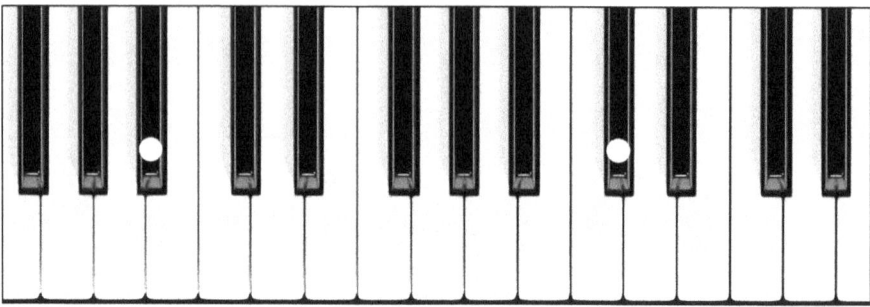

Figure 9.8 - Example of a black to black minor tenth I can play on a DS5.5 keyboard.

White to white tenths also are playable:

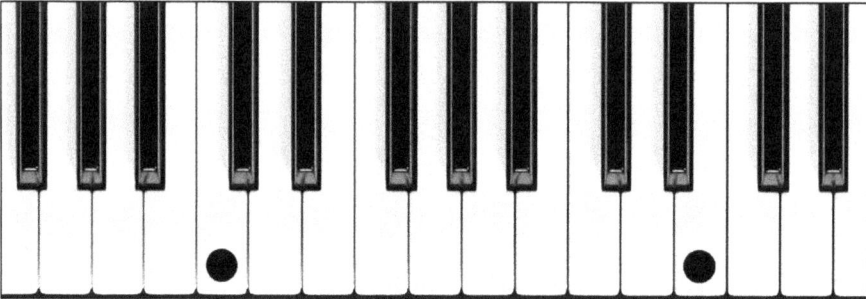

Figure 9.9 - Example of a white to white major tenths I can play on a DS5.5 keyboard.

However, I have a problem with white to black and black to white tenths. The white to black tenths are barely playable and require my absolute full stretch:

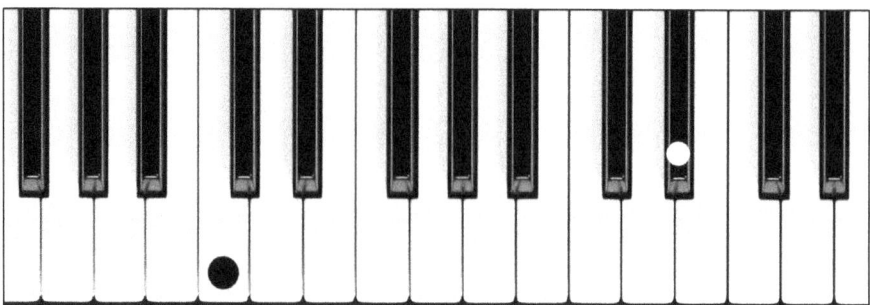

Figure 9.10 - Example of a white to black minor tenth that is barely playable by me on a DS5.5 keyboard.

The even larger black to white tenths are unreachable in my right hand (as they mostly are in my left as well):

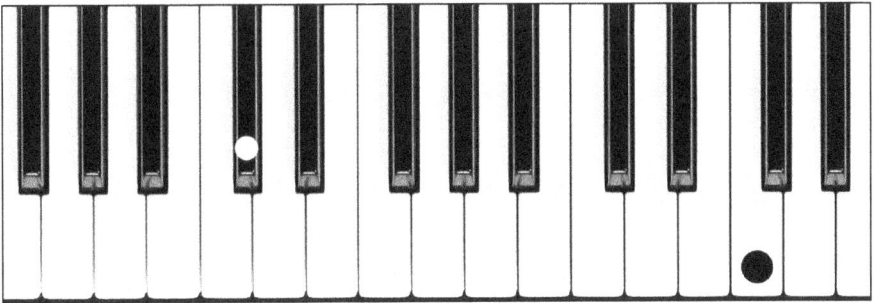

Figure 9.11 - Example of a black to white major tenth I am unable to play on a DS5.5 keyboard.

I rarely play fuller chords with tenths in the right hand, but as discussed in Chapter 4, the Count Basie ending phrase is something I do play relatively often, and it uses filled-in tenth chords. On the DS5.5 keyboard I can play it in some keys, in other keys with difficulty, and there are a few keys in which I can't really play it at all.

In summary, I am in Zone B on the hand span chart, and a DS5.5 keyboard effectively moves me well into Zone C. It's really a miracle, and most people would be satisfied with that vast improvement in reach, comfort, and capability.

I was aspiring to emulate Oscar Peterson, however, and his hands were well into Zone D. He had no difficulty playing any of the chords and voicings I've presented as still being a challenge to me on the DS5.5. I came to the conclusion that while a DS5.5 keyboard would get me 90% of the way there and would be useful in almost all scenarios, if I really wanted to reach my ultimate goals, especially in playing solo jazz piano, I was going to need an even narrower keyboard.

But I wasn't sure just how narrow to go. Reducing the width of the keyboard increasingly introduces new problems. As the keys become narrower, the black keys move much closer together, making it increasingly difficult to fit fingers between them.

I had been strongly considering having David Steinbuhler retrofit a narrower keyboard into the Kawai MP11SE. Steinbuhler can customize his keyboards to any size, not just the DS Standard sizes. Since I wasn't certain what my optimal size would be, I thought it would be useful at this point to talk to him in person, play on his keyboards, and try to come to a decision.

MEETING DAVID STEINBUHLER

Early in 2023 I scheduled a visit to Titusville, PA to meet David Steinbuhler and try out his narrower keyboards. This was an experience I will never forget–I was finally in the presence of one of the pioneers who made all of this possible.

David started me on the DS6.0 keyboard. I adjusted to the smaller size immediately without even having to think about it. I found I could now reach some of the tenths, although they required my maximum stretch. But playing tunes that are strenuous for me on a conventional DS6.5 keyboard was much more comfortable on the DS6.0. Even though I didn't have the full reach I wanted, it was more comfortable playing what I was accustomed to playing with my limited reach. I didn't play on the DS6.0 keyboard for long because I wanted to move on to the narrower keyboards, which I knew were more appropriately sized for me.

David switched out the DS6.0 and put in the DS5.5 keyboard. This keyboard was very comfortable for me. I felt like it brought me 85-90% of the way to where I wanted to be, just like I had found on the small Korg keyboard. The only things that were still beyond my reach were some of the largest tenths in the left hand and full tenth chords in the left hand with fifths and/or sevenths included (in every key). In addition, filled-in tenth chords in the right hand were playable, but only with limited power and comfort, and I had difficulty playing faster walking tenths in the left hand. Other than that, the DS5.5 was the right size for me. I played on it for 30-45 minutes. We then switched to the DS5.1–the child-size keyboard.

I placed my hands on the keyboard, and I was amazed by what I saw. Even more than the DS5.5, the DS5.1 made my hands feel big. But even on this keyboard, they were not oversized. As I started to play some chords, I realized that for the first time in my life, my hands were actually optimally-sized for the keyboard I was playing. The keyboard fit my hands in the same way and with the same proportions that a conventional keyboard fits the hands of someone like Oscar Peterson.

I felt like I could have complete control over the instrument through the DS5.1 keyboard, and I started to experiment with it. I played a major scale just to get the feel for an octave. Then I played some tenth chords in my left hand. To my amazement, I actually overshot one of the tenths and played an eleventh instead. That did not mean my hand was too big for the keyboard. It meant I could play those big tenth chords continuously without any strain or pain because rather than requiring my full reach, I could play with a more relaxed hand no matter how widely the chord was spread out (and how thickly it was filled in). I played around with walking tenths in my left hand using my fourth finger to create a legato feel–I could do that! I could also play large tenth chords in the right hand and had much more power at my disposal playing those big chords and intervals.

As I started to play some actual tunes, I realized that I was going to need to re-learn how to play the piano in many ways.

The one limitation I found on the DS5.1 keyboard was that my middle finger was a little too thick to fit between the black keys. That's a problem I would address about a year later, and I will discuss that process in Chapter 10.

DS5.1: THE KEYS THAT FIT

When you first look at a DS5.1 (or even a DS5.5) keyboard, the keys look unusually narrow because you're so used to the conventional DS6.5 keyboard. I found that if I thought of the keyboard being normal–this is the way it's supposed to look–then my hands and fingers would naturally find what they needed to play. Yes, I overshot octaves and other intervals for a while, and yes, my play was a bit sloppy as I figured out how my hands should fit on the keyboard. But in the short time I played with the keyboard, I was able to get by pretty well. And given a few days to settle into this keyboard, I could tell I would feel right at home. There were no more limitations–everything I wanted to do was within reach, and it felt like this keyboard opened a whole world of possibilities for me. This is the size for me. I'm a

DS5.1 player.

For a typical Zone B player, the DS5.5 is the right size keyboard. But for a Zone B player who is partial to playing Oscar Peterson's music (i.e., me), the keys on the DS5.5 are not narrow enough.

I think David was surprised by my preference for the DS5.1. The DS5.5 keyboard places me firmly in Zone C, effectively classifying me as a large-handed pianist. Still, he understood and respected my reasons for choosing the even narrower size.

When we finished up with the various narrower keyboards, I turned around and looked at the keyboard on the upright piano sitting behind me. It was a conventional DS6.5 keyboard. Those keys looked absurdly–almost comically–large to me. How is anyone supposed to play this?, I thought. Then I looked back at the DS5.1–and it looked just right.

MY OSCAR PETERSON-SIZED HANDS

I once had the opportunity to shake Oscar Peterson's hand. He was well into Zone D with his huge hands that could likely reach a twelfth on the conventional keyboard. I'll never forget the feeling. It felt like my "child hand" was being swallowed up inside his!

Let's take a look at the hand span images from Chapter 4, where I compared Oscar Peterson's hands to my hands on the conventional keyboard. Remember how small my hands looked compared to his? Now let's revisit that comparison with my hands on the DS5.1 keyboard. Figure 9.12 shows the estimated hand span of Oscar Peterson on a conventional keyboard. Figure 9.13 shows my hand span on a conventional keyboard. And Figure 9.14 shows my hand span on a DS5.1 keyboard. For ease of comparison, Figure 9.14 is scaled so that the keyboard has the same width as it does in the other two figures.

These figures reveal that my hands on a DS5.1 keyboard look very similar to Oscar Peterson's hands on a conventional DS6.5 keyboard. I have only slightly less reach than Oscar had, and I am able to play all of the chords and intervals that are still unreachable for me on a DS5.5 keyboard.

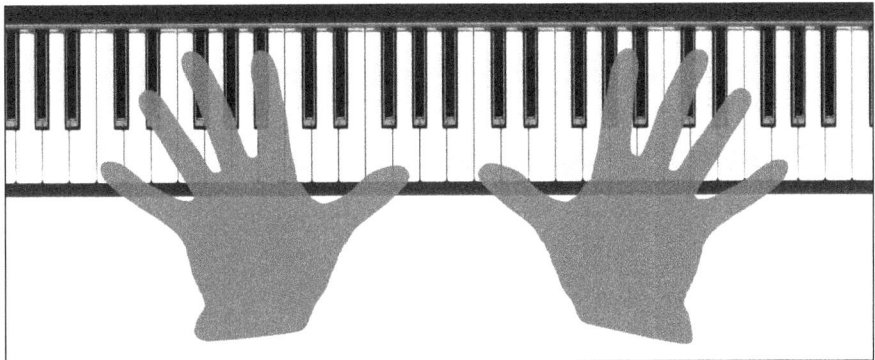

Figure 9.12 - Oscar Peterson's hands (estimated) on conventional keyboard.

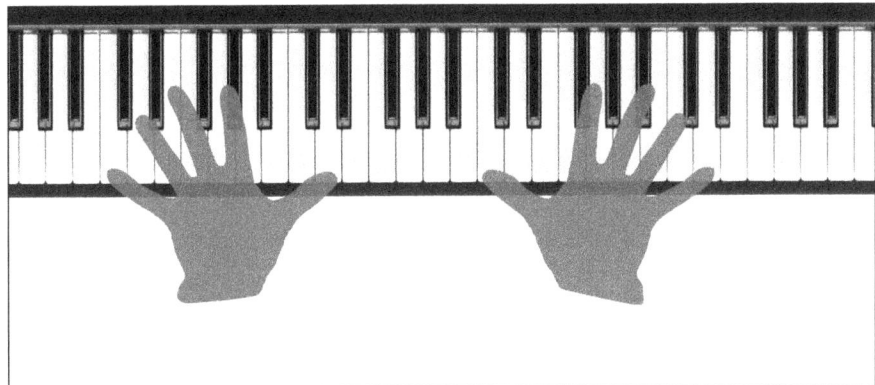

Figure 9.13 - My hands on conventional keyboard.

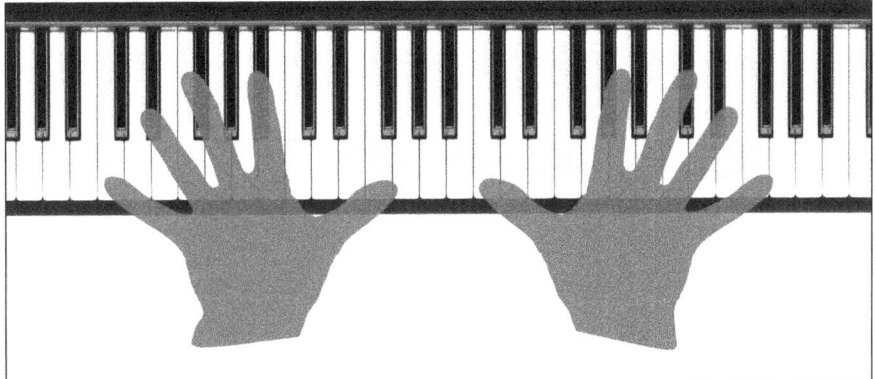

Figure 9.14 - My hands on a DS5.1 keyboard. This image has been scaled so the keyboard width matches the conventional keyboard in the figures above for comparison.

Now let's look at real keyboards. This is what my hand looks like playing an octave on the conventional keyboard:

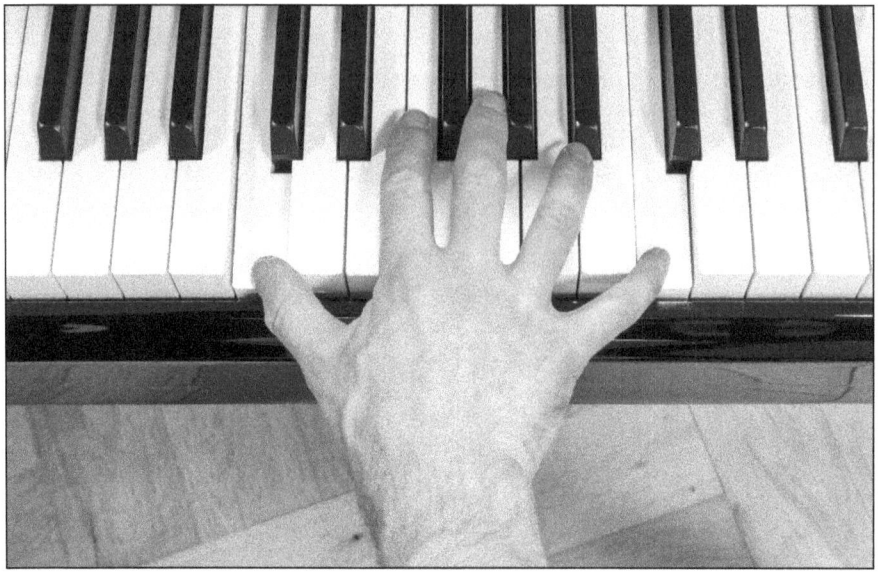

Figure 9.15 - My hand playing an octave on a conventional keyboard.

Compare this to my hand playing an octave on a DS5.1 keyboard, and observe how much more comfortable and relaxed it looks on the narrower keyboard:

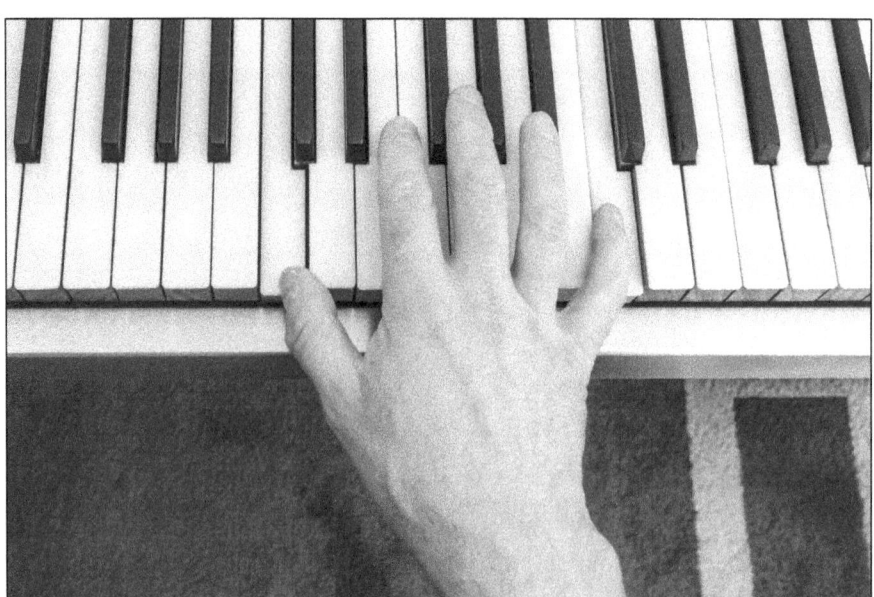

Figure 9.16 - My hand playing an octave on a DS5.1 keyboard.

Finally, here is what my hand looks like playing a large, filled-in tenth chord on the DS5.1 keyboard:

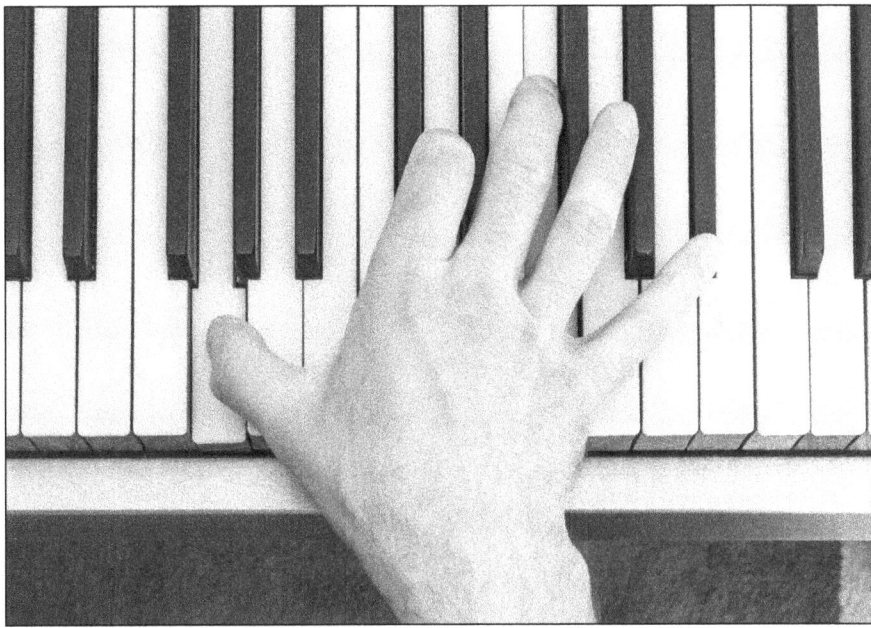

Figure 9.17 - My hand playing a large chord with a tenth on a DS5.1 keyboard.

This is why I've settled on the DS5.1 for my use. I now play a digital piano that is designed with 5.1 inches per octave. The key design has been customized to eliminate some of the issues that develop with such a small keyboard, specifically the space between the black keys. With this instrument, I am effectively in Zone D, with no physical limitations whatsoever on the music I play. For this I have a very special company to thank, Kaduk Musical Instruments.

But what is Kaduk Musical Instruments, and how did I come to acquire my instrument from them? We'll cover that story in the next chapter.

Chapter 10

KADUK MUSICAL INSTRUMENTS

Creating the Perfect Fit

In 2024, having determined to acquire a DS5.1 digital keyboard, I began investigating the options available to me. For the past year I had been on David Steinbuhler's waiting list for a retrofit of the Kawai MP11SE, but there were many other customers ahead of me on the list. Also, David had mentioned there were a few technical issues to work out for the digital retrofit, so it was not going to be straightforward. I was concerned that this process could take years, and I didn't want to wait that long, so I began researching other options.

INITIAL INVESTIGATIONS

I started by contacting a number of individuals and companies to investigate the possibilities of the same retrofit David Steinbuhler was to design for me, or to build a completely new instrument with a DS5.1 keyboard.

I spoke with David Rubenstein from Los Angeles, a piano restorer and builder of unique instruments. He was confident he could retrofit a DS5.1 keyboard into the Kawai digital piano but expressed concerns about potential complications, noting that the DS5.1 size is at the extreme edge of feasibility. He advised me to continue waiting for David Steinbuhler and suggested that if things didn't progress within a reasonable time frame, I could reach out to him again. I came away feeling reasonably confident that he could complete the retrofit; the main uncertainty was the final cost, which would depend on any complications he encountered once he began the work. In any case, it would be a long wait.

I contacted one other custom piano maker similar to David Rubenstein, but he felt it would be too much research and design for him to make it work.

Next, I reached out to Vidal, a small start-up developing a new digital MIDI keyboard featuring wooden keys and an inertial action. The instrument appeared impressive, designed to play and feel remarkably similar to a traditional piano. Since Vidal engineered the product from the ground up, I was confident they had the expertise to create a custom-sized keyboard. When I inquired about this possibility, however, they replied that it would require extensive development and was not something they intended to pursue at this time.

I also considered PianoArc, the company behind the NK 5.5, developed in partnership with Narrow Keys. I had previously met with their team when addressing a minor issue with my NK 5.5. During those conversations, I mentioned my interest in an "NK 5.1." While I believe PianoArc could produce it, I had the impression that doing so would demand significant design modifications to the NK 5.5. Currently, Narrow Keys is focused on offering the DS5.5 size, as it benefits the largest group of pianists. If they were to add another size, it would most likely be DS6.0. I never formally asked PianoArc about a DS5.1 keyboard–considering it would be best to raise the request through Narrow Keys. But I continued to see it as a possibility for the future.

The final option I was aware of was developed by Kaduk Musical Instruments in The Netherlands (now based in Poland). Kaduk is a pioneering design and development company specializing in the creation of innovative, custom, and modular musical instruments, with a strong focus on piano technology. Their main work focuses on empowering musicians through the integration of advanced scientific, ergonomic, and aesthetic principles into instrument construction.[87]

Kaduk specializes in retrofitting acoustic pianos with custom-made ergonomic keyboards using advanced automated computer-aided design and manufacturing technology. Their retrofit services allow for both grand and upright acoustic pianos to be equipped with keyboards of any size or ergonomic specification, tailored to the individual needs of the player.[88]

On the digital side, Kaduk developed Respons, an innovative digital piano instrument that operates as a true ballistic instrument (like an acoustic piano) rather than relying on velocity sensors like traditional digital instruments. An acoustic piano's sound is produced by the ballistic action of a hammer striking the strings. When a key is pressed, the pianist's finger initiates a swift, forceful motion that causes the hammer to rapidly hit the string. In contrast, traditional digital pianos use velocity sensors to measure how much force the player applies to the key. In Respons, Kaduk has replaced these velocity-based sensors with a ballistic system similar to an acoustic action.

The use of ballistic sensors enables the instrument to feel and play more like an acoustic piano than has been possible in any digital piano before it. Even the Kawai MP11SE, which essentially has a full piano action built into it–including simulated hammers–ultimately relies on velocity sensors and therefore can never fully duplicate the feel and response of a real piano action. Respons was designed to capture subtle nuances and unique vibrational patterns of each keystroke, translating them into rich, varied sound for a highly expressive playing experience. And the Respons was designed to be made with any size keys down to three quarters size, or 4.875 inches per octave.[89]

The Respons appeared to be the ideal option for me, but more than a year after it was announced, it was still not in production. When I

---

[87] "Home." *Kaduk Musical Instruments,* https://www.kaduk.nl/. Accessed July 28, 2025.
[88] Ibid.
[89] "Respons." *Kaduk Musical Instruments,* https://www.kaduk.nl/flagship-projects/respons. Accessed July 28, 2025.

contacted Kaduk to inquire about the delay, they responded that, unfortunately, they were unable to obtain the specialized chips needed for the manufacturing process. There was no estimated timeframe for when production would begin. This did not sound promising, and I considered this a dead end for my search.

THOMAS KADUK

As it turned out, it wasn't a dead end after all. Several weeks later, I received an email from Thomas Kaduk himself, the founder of Kaduk Musical Instruments. He wanted to know if I was still interested in his company's digital instruments. I explained my interest in the retrofit to the Kawai keyboard, but that what I really preferred was the Respons. He suggested we set up a video call to discuss the options.

Rather than retrofitting a Kawai instrument, Thomas asked, why not build something new from scratch? While he was unable to produce the Respons piano, Thomas matter-of-factly said he could easily produce a traditional, velocity sensor-based instrument in a short period of time. He explained that he could build a brand new, custom digital piano for me, with a keyboard of any size I desired. I was completely floored by this idea. But commissioning a one-of-a-kind instrument had to be prohibitively expensive, didn't it? To my surprise, the cost was actually comparable to purchasing and retrofitting the Kawai MP11SE. It seemed I had finally found what I had been looking for!

Working with Thomas Kaduk quickly proved to be the perfect decision for me. His knowledge of piano actions and keyboard design is extensive, and he has the technology to design a keyboard at any size, customized to certain hand measurements. He can make keyboards in the DS Standard sizes, but he prefers to measure the player's hands and design a keyboard that is optimally suited to the individual. I wanted a 5.1-inch octave, but my fingers are too thick to fit between the black keys at that size. Thomas had me take some measurements of my hands and fingers. Based on those measurements he suggested a keyboard layout that provided enough space between the black keys for my fingers while keeping the overall octave width to 132 mm (5.2 inches). The next day he provided a digital 3D model I could view, measure, and print on paper.

We further customized the design because I wanted to decrease how high the black keys rise above the white keys. You can see what I mean in Figure 10.1, a photograph of the keyboard on my finished instrument. Since all of the keys are so much narrower, I wanted to decrease this height so that the space between the black keys wouldn't feel so much like a deep canyon, and that would help with any remaining issue fitting my fingers between those keys. We discussed the trade-offs with making this change and ultimately settled on a design to achieve some reduction in height without sacrificing control or power.

Figure 10.1 - Keyboard on my Kaduk digital piano. Note the proportional height of the black keys above the white keys.[90]

Thomas had a 3D print of the design made and delivered to me for evaluation. I decided the keyboard layout would work, however I preferred the keyboard width to be all the way down to 5.1 inches per octave rather than 5.2 inches. At a size of 132 mm (5.2 inches), I could reach every chord, but some were still slightly uncomfortable. Having played on David Steinbuhler's DS5.1 keyboard, I knew that an extra tenth of an inch per octave would make all the difference in my feeling comfortable with the largest chords. But I did not want to change the

[90] Photograph by the author.

width of the black keys or decrease the distance between them, because we had already optimized those dimensions.

I suggested we shave 0.5 mm off all the B, C, E, and F white keys, where there is no black key in between them (refer to the piano diagram in Figure 1.1 on page 6). That reduction would be essentially unnoticeable on the individual keys but would reduce the octave width to 130 mm (just about 5.1 inches) without affecting the black key widths or distances except where there is a large gap. It would save more than 2.5 mm when playing large chords with tenths. Although this would take some manual work on their part and additional cost, it is something Thomas was able to do.

Extra Keys

During our collaboration, I had one more idea in the back of my mind, and I finally worked up the courage to ask Thomas about this additional customization. To produce the sound from my computer, I use the Synchron Bösendorfer Imperial sample library from Vienna Symphonic Library–a magnificent and thorough sampling of the 9-foot Bösendorfer Imperial concert grand piano in a well-controlled studio/concert hall setting. The Bösendorfer Imperial has 9 extra bass keys, taking the piano all the way down to bottom C, and the VSL Synchron library includes samples of these extra sub-bass notes. Unless you shift the octave either on your MIDI controller or in the software, however, you can't take advantage of these notes with an 88-key controller.

We were building my instrument from scratch, so I figured it would be worth asking Thomas if it would be possible to add nine extra keys in my instrument. The answer was yes, but it would take additional design effort and of course the materials, so it would add cost to the instrument. As you can see in Figure 10.2, Thomas designed the extra bass keys all to have black tops, just like on the Bösendorfer Imperial. This prevents visual confusion since the player is so accustomed to the keyboard ending on an A.

After the additional customization and accounting for shipping and currency exchange rates, the price was only slightly more than a Kawai retrofit. I gave the green light to start development, made a deposit, and a little over six months later my instrument was ready to ship.

Figure 10.2 - Extra bass keys on Kaduk piano.[91]

It took considerably less than six months to actually build the instrument. But as this was the first of its kind, Thomas wanted to put it through extensive testing and give pianists in Europe an opportunity to play it so he could identify any issues that might take more time to surface. The feedback he received from the European pianists, including both professionals and amateurs, was very positive. In one case Thomas told me a pianist said he wanted to trade in his Steinway piano for my instrument!

The Sea Voyage

Once my piano was ready to deliver to me, Thomas faced the challenge of arranging shipment from Poland to the United States. The most practical solution was to send it as freight aboard a container ship. My piano took a month-long journey halfway around the world

---

[91] Photograph by the author.

by sea, and I was able to track its progress at every stage on a website that gathers and maps the Automatic Identification System (AIS) transponder signals of ships around the world.

The instrument traveled on the *NYK Daedalus,* crossing the Atlantic Ocean, passing through the Panama Canal, and finally arriving at the Port of Los Angeles. I worked closely with a customs broker to ensure everything was cleared properly and all tariffs and fees were settled. Early in 2025, my new digital piano was finally delivered to my home. The thrill of unboxing it and setting it up in my living room is difficult to put into words.

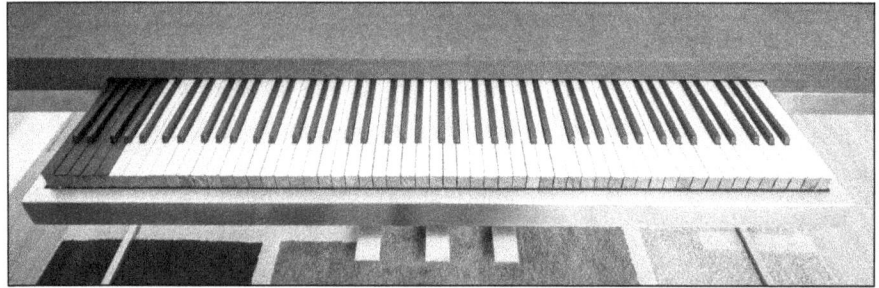

Figure 10.3 - 97-key digital piano keyboard from Kaduk Musical Instruments.[92]

Thanks to Thomas Kaduk's ability to customize a keyboard design and a digital instrument, I now have what is for me the ultimate digital piano. In just six months, it has propelled my jazz piano skills farther than I managed to progress in the previous six years. I love this instrument. It is beautiful, it is extremely well-built, and it is a dream to play. I really cannot describe the feeling of playing this instrument. While I don't often make use of those extra bass notes, it's satisfying having them there. Playing the Synchron Bösendorfer Imperial sample library feels realistic because of its outstanding sound, and playing it on a keyboard that has those nine extra bass keys adds even more to that realism. It truly feels like I'm playing the 9 foot Imperial. And best of all, it is a piano that is perfectly designed to fit my hands.

---

[92] Photograph by the author.

THE FAIRKEY STANDALONE DIGITAL CUSTOM FIT PIANO

Shortly after my instrument was completed, Kaduk began marketing the piano as the Fairkey Standalone Digital Custom Fit Piano on their Fairkey.direct website. This piano is the result of Thomas Kaduk's ongoing research and development, and my instrument was the first of its kind to be made.

Figure 10.4 - The first Fairkey Standalone Digital Custom Fit Piano.[93]

Fairkey.direct offers an innovative range of customizable piano keyboards, both digital and acoustic, designed to prioritize ergonomics and accommodate pianists of all hand sizes. Fairkey.direct helps users take accurate hand measurements through a fully guided and remote measurement system designed to be foolproof and easy to use. Their system calculates the optimal keyboard layout based on how the user's hand actually works, rather than just static

---

[93] Photograph by the author.

measurements on paper. To assist with this process, Fairkey provides free downloadable measurement tools that guide users step-by-step in measuring key aspects of their hands, such as finger spacing and finger-to-finger distances, which are critical for customizing the key widths and spacing.[94]

This approach allows Fairkey to tailor the piano keyboard dimensions, including key width, spacing, and overall keyboard size, to each player's hand geometry, creating an ergonomic fit that reduces strain and optimizes playability. By focusing on the individual pianist's physical needs and musical ambitions rather than traditional one-size-fits-all standards, Fairkey.direct opens new possibilities for comfort and expressive freedom in piano performance.[95]

"Anything Is Possible"

At various points during my discussions with Thomas Kaduk, when I asked about certain features or changes, Thomas would pause and then invariably respond with something like, "of course anything is possible–we just need to think about how to do it." In a world in which pianists seeking alternative keyboard sizes have been repeatedly told "no" for decades by traditional piano and digital piano manufacturers, or "that's not something we're interested in doing", or "that's not possible", or "that would never work", "it would be too expensive", "there's no market for it", etc., etc., how refreshing it was to encounter someone whose first instinct was to say, "yes, that is possible and we will figure out how to do it"!

Thomas Kaduk's knowledge and experience with piano keyboards and actions are impressive. Over years of designing retrofit keyboards for acoustic instruments and researching and designing prototype digital piano systems, Thomas has acquired a unique and deep understanding of piano technology. He understands both the physics and the practical applications of mechanical actions

---

[94] "Fairkey-direct." *ergonomic piano keyboards,* https://www.fairkey.direct/. Accessed July 25, 2025.
[95] Ibid.

and sound production. I am proud to have worked with Thomas Kaduk to produce my custom digital piano, and the instrument brings me joy every time I play it. I am so grateful for our working relationship and the friendship we developed.

Chapter 11

THE NEW NORMAL

Leveling the Playing Field

For over two years, I've been playing exclusively on narrower keyboards, a DS5.5 and a DS5.1 keyboard. I have had no need nor desire to play a conventional DS6.5 keyboard since then. As described in Chapter 7, one objection some people make about becoming accustomed to narrower keyboards is that they will no longer be able to play on the conventional size keyboard. That could be a concern for people who play in public regularly and need to play on the piano that is available to them, which almost certainly has a conventional DS6.5 keyboard. For people like me who either don't play away from home or bring their own keyboard when they do, there is no need to worry about having to play on a conventional keyboard. Even among those who have no choice, the collective experience of pianists who regularly use and prefer narrower keyboards consistently shows that adapting between keyboard sizes is not a problem.

But none of these or any of the other common objections discussed in Chapter 7 really matter. At the end of the day, when you sit down to the piano, you either feel comfortable, or you don't. And unless you have size alternatives, you may never even realize how uncomfortable you actually are. However, if you have smaller hands and are used to a narrower keyboard, the next time you sit down at a conventional keyboard you will say to yourself, this is absurdly too big for me.

I was recently photographing a luxury hotel suite for an architecture client. When I entered, the first thing that caught my attention was a grand piano in the middle of the room. I opened the keyboard, curious about its sound quality and whether the instrument was well-maintained. I hadn't looked at a conventional DS6.5 keyboard in person in at least six months. I must say, the keyboard looked absolutely ridiculous to me. It looked like some kind of cartoon. I put my hands on the keyboard and realized I had to stretch just to reach a ninth. I played a few notes and felt how much more force is required to play these keys than what was needed with my own keyboard.

As I looked at my small hands on this conventional DS6.5 keyboard, I wondered how I went through so many years of pain and frustration without realizing how unnecessary it was. Nobody with smaller hands should be playing a keyboard this size. It's so clear to me now, and seeing my small hands on a large keyboard again reinforced the impact this experience has had on my musical life.

After some initial adjustment–I hadn't played a conventional-sized keyboard in more than two years–I found I could play this piano again. The mechanics came back quickly, along with that old, familiar tension and constant strain I used to accept as normal. It's remarkable how easily you grow accustomed to discomfort, often without even noticing it.

But now, having experienced something better, I knew what I was missing. I could physically play this piano, but I couldn't truly play the music I wanted. The satisfaction just wasn't there. In truth, it was frustrating. This keyboard felt as if it was holding me back, robbing me of my ability to express my full capabilities.

I am deeply grateful for my DS5.5 and DS5.1 keyboards and for the people who made them possible. For many years I understood my limitations on the conventional keyboard, but the extent of musical freedom and joy I've discovered with these narrower keyboards was beyond anything I could have imagined.

Narrower keyboards are common sense. Once you have played on narrower keyboards, it is so profoundly obvious that it becomes difficult to understand how anyone could seriously tell you otherwise. You just look at them dumbfounded, thinking "what is wrong with this person?"

GOLIATH KEYBOARD CHALLENGE

All of this is especially difficult for people with larger hands to understand. They are the people most likely to think that one size fits all–this works for me, why wouldn't it work for anyone else?

One way to demonstrate the feeling of playing an over-sized keyboard is through the "Goliath keyboard challenge." The PASK website makes available 3D keyboard models sized at 7.6 inches per octave to give people a feel for how the conventional keyboard feels to smaller-handed players.[96]

But in the context of a book, I can demonstrate this to you by using the hand and piano diagrams we've looked at in earlier chapters. Let's take a look at the average Zone C player's hands on a piano with a 7.68-inch octave rather than the conventional 6.5-inch octave. The increase from a 6.5-inch to a 7.68-inch octave is comparable to the increase from the 5.5-inch to the 6.5-inch octave. Here's what that would look like:

---

[96] Resources & links." *Pianists for Alternatively Sized Keyboards,* https://paskpiano.org/resources-and-links/. Accessed July 21, 2025.

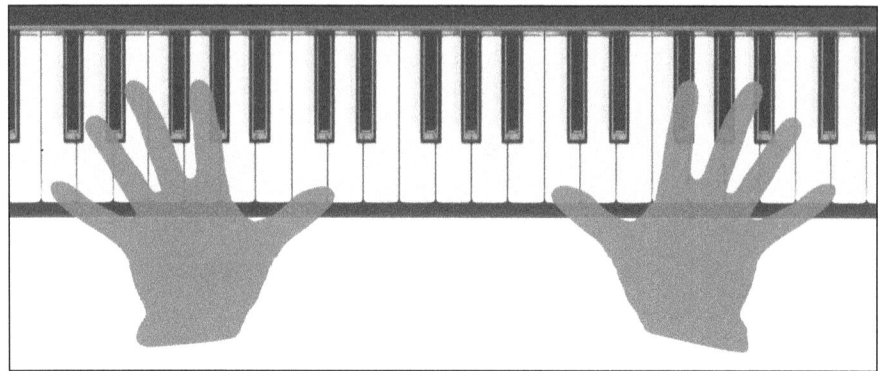

Figure 11.1 - Zone C "large" hands on a 7.68 inches per octave keyboard.

These hands don't look so big any more, and in fact, they would be considered small. Notice how they cannot cleanly play a ninth. We can take this a step further. Now let's imagine increasing the keyboard width further to 8.28 inches per octave. The increase from a 6.5-inch to an 8.28-inch octave is comparable to the increase from the 5.1-inch to the 6.5-inch octave. Let's look at Oscar Peterson's hands (a Zone D player) on this much larger keyboard in Figure 11.2.

Even Oscar Peterson's hands would be limited to a ninth on this scaled-up piano keyboard. Imagine that–Oscar Peterson, renowned for his virtuosity, suddenly facing the limitations of small hands. Remember my allusion to *Jack and the Beanstalk* in the introduction to this book? If the world were populated by giants and this over-sized keyboard were the standard, Oscar Peterson would be forced to seek out a much narrower DS6.5 keyboard. In such a scenario, it's uncertain whether an alternative like the DS6.5 would even exist. Christopher Donison used to end his talks on narrower keyboards by holding up his hands and declaring that if the renowned classical pianist Vladimir Horowitz had been born with these hands, we never would have heard of him.[97] Similarly, in this hypothetical world of giants, Oscar Peterson's hands would likely have held him back to the point that we never would have heard of him as a jazz pianist. Consider the musical loss we would have suffered, all because the keyboard was too large for his hands to realize his full potential at the piano.

---

[97] Donison, Christopher. "DS Keyboard." *Christopher Donison,* http://www.chrisdonison.com/keyboard.html. Accessed July 16, 2025.

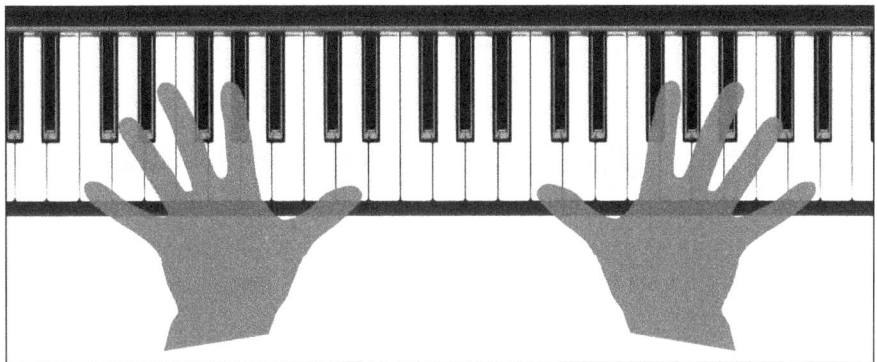

Figure 11.2 - Oscar Peterson's Zone D "very large" hands on an 8.28 per inch octave keyboard

If Zone C or Zone D players encountered a keyboard this large, their immediate reaction would likely be disbelief–wondering how anyone could possibly play it. The instrument would appear absurdly over-sized, with keys that seem cartoonish in their proportions. They would quickly discover they could no longer play the repertoire they're accustomed to; instead, they'd feel frustration and even pain as they strained to reach intervals that now push their hands to the limit. Sound familiar? The diagrams here can't fully capture this reality–the scaling of the images I've had to use for the purposes of this book makes it hard to convey just how over-sized such a keyboard would look and feel. Trust me, in person, it's unmistakably and almost comically large.

For many, this thought experiment may be hard to fully grasp. The only truly convincing evidence would be to encounter a keyboard with a 7.68- or 8.28-inch octave in real life. Speaking from personal experience–since this is exactly how the DS6.5 keyboard feels to me–there's really no other possible reaction than outright objection. Only by confronting such an instrument firsthand can someone truly understand what I, and many other pianists, experience every day.

Fortunately for Zone C and Zone D players, the conventional keyboard measures just 6.5 inches per octave. And for those of us in

Zones A and B–the majority–we no longer have to accept the DS6.5 as our only option.

This is the new normal. With my DS5.1 and DS5.5 keyboards, I'm finally able to achieve the level of musical expression I've always aspired to.

EPILOGUE

As I look back on this journey, from my first encounters with the limitations of conventional piano keyboards to the thrill of discovering instruments tailored for hands like mine, I am filled with both gratitude and a sense of possibility. What began as quiet frustration and doubt slowly transformed into hope, then determination, and finally, into the realization of musical freedom I'd only ever dreamed of.

The search for a piano that truly fits is, at its core, a search for self-expression without barriers. Along the way, I encountered skepticism, technical challenges, and moments of uncertainty. But I also found a community of passionate advocates, visionary builders, and fellow pianists who refuse to accept that artistry should be limited by tradition alone.

Every step–researching alternative keyboard sizes, reaching out to manufacturers, and working with craftsmen across continents–has deepened my appreciation for what's possible when design meets the diversity of human hands. The day my own narrower keyboard arrived was more than a milestone in piano ownership; it was the start of a new chapter in my musical life.

Now, as I sit at my instrument with my fingers on the chords and passages that were once completely out of reach, I am reminded that change in the arts often comes at a personal level: one story, one innovation, one converted skeptic at a time. My experience stands as just one voice among many, adding to a growing chorus calling for more inclusive, ergonomic approaches in piano design.

My hope is that this book has not only chronicled my personal evolution, but also sparked a vision of what's possible: a world in which pianists of all hand sizes can pursue their artistry without compromise.

Here's to music that feels truly within reach, literally and figuratively, and to the ongoing journey of discovery, for all of us who dare to imagine a more accessible keyboard, and a more expressive future.

ACKNOWLEDGMENTS

Writing a book is rarely a solitary endeavor–even though much of the work takes place alone. I am deeply grateful to the colleagues, friends, and family who offered advice, encouragement, and insight along the way.

My heartfelt thanks go to Rhonda Boyle, both for graciously agreeing to write the foreword to this book and for her decades-long dedication to advancing narrower keyboards. The PASK website, which she manages, served as a vital resource in my research, and her own pioneering work on hand spans was central to my arguments in favor of alternative keyboard sizes.

I am equally indebted to Dr. Carol Leone, who not only read an early draft of this book and provided thoughtful suggestions, but also gave me a formative musical experience more than twenty years ago by inviting me into her office at SMU to play her DS5.5 piano–my very first encounter with narrower keyboards.

I also wish to thank Jeremy Siskind for nurturing my continued growth as a jazz pianist, and for his generosity in allowing me to quote from his work and reproduce his shared-hand voicings diagram.

I extend my sincere gratitude to Linda Gould for her prompt and informative responses to my inquiries regarding her initial experience with David Steinbuhler's prototype keyboard. I am also deeply thankful to Linda Gould and Kathy Strauch for their pioneering efforts in advancing narrower digital keyboards at affordable prices.

In 2023, David Steinbuhler welcomed me into his home and offered the rare opportunity to explore a variety of narrow keyboards for several hours. I remain grateful for his warmth, hospitality, and the more than three remarkable decades he has devoted to building, refining, and making these instruments available to so many.

In 2024, I had the privilege of collaborating with Thomas Kaduk to create my custom narrower digital keyboard. I am thankful for his understanding, ingenuity, and can-do spirit, which resulted in an instrument that fits my hands perfectly.

Finally, I owe a special debt of gratitude to my editor–and my sister, Ellen Scholnicoff–for her diligence, keen eye, and perceptive suggestions, which made this book clearer, more engaging, and more approachable for a wide audience. More importantly, I am grateful for her unwavering support, her belief in this project, and for her being the best sister I could ever hope for.

For More Information

The movement in support of alternative size piano keyboards continues to grow. More and more pianists are turning to narrower keyboards to alleviate their pain and to open up a new world of musical possibilities for themselves. There are a number of people and organizations who have worked tirelessly to get us to this point, and who continue to advocate for narrower keyboards. Here's a brief overview of what's going on in the narrow keys piano world right now and where you can find more information.

PASK

Pianists for Alternatively Sized Keyboards (PASK) is an active community of piano teachers and students, professional pianists, acoustic and digital piano manufacturers, and piano technicians. It serves as a hub for all activity relating to alternative size keyboards.

The PASK website, https://paskpiano.org/ offers a wealth of information on narrower keyboards, including history, research, personal testimonials, and links to additional resources. I have relied heavily on the resources of the PASK website in putting this book together.

The PASK organization also hosts a lively Facebook group where members can share stories, notify each other of upcoming events, and hold discussions on any topic relating to narrow piano keyboards.

INTERNATIONAL STRETTO PIANO FESTIVAL

The International Stretto Piano Festival, founded by Hannah Reimann, is dedicated to the advancement of narrower, or stretto (Italian for narrow) piano keyboards. For the past five years, the festival has organized international concerts featuring musicians playing on any keyboard narrower than the conventional DS6.5 size. The events are designed to highlight exceptional artistry while promoting awareness of the importance of hand-size accommodation in piano playing. Accomplished pianists from around the world participate and perform using alternative-sized keyboards.

For more information, visit their website at https://www.strettopianoconcerts.org/.

SIRIUS 6.0 PIANOS

The Future Initiative SIRIUS 6.0, launched in 2020 at the Staatliche Hochschule für Musik und Darstellende Kunst Stuttgart (HMDK Stuttgart), focuses on the exchange of experiences, dissemination, and further development of piano keyboards with narrower keys, specifically those measuring 6.0 inches per octave. Positioned at the intersection of piano performance, music physiology, and musician health, the initiative aims to expand artistic potential through ergonomically improved keyboard designs that reduce playing strain, increase precision, enrich tonal control, and promote gender equality and injury prevention among pianists.[98]

After a four-year pilot phase with a prototype, the initiative successfully inaugurated Europe's first interchangeable SIRIUS 6.0 keyboard for a Steinway D concert grand piano in spring 2024. Since then, several music institutions including Hochschule für Musik Nürnberg, Tiroler Landeskonservatorium Innsbruck, and Hochschule für Musik und Theater München have joined the initiative, integrating SIRIUS 6.0 keyboards into their programs. Notably, in 2024 the German Pension Insurance approved funding for a SIRIUS 6.0 keyboard as a workplace technical aid for a professional pianist, marking a significant milestone for musician health and accessibility.[99]

The initiative's impact is also showcased through collaborations with piano manufacturers and partner institutions. In 2024, the Hochschule für Musik Nürnberg adopted the SIRIUS 6.0 keyboard on a Steinway M, while the interchangeable action for the Steinway D at HMDK Stuttgart was produced in cooperation with Kluge and Steinway & Sons Hamburg, enabling pianists to switch easily between standard and narrower keyboards during concerts and recitals.[100]

The initiative's public engagement includes educational outreach via the Stretto Piano Festival (see above), as well as video series sharing user experiences. The Future Initiative SIRIUS 6.0 merges scientific research, instrument innovation, and community activism to foster equal opportunity and health-conscious piano playing across Europe and beyond.

See the footnotes for links to more information on SIRIUS 6.0.

---

[98] Stöger, M. (February 2024). *SIRIUS 6.0 – Klaviaturen, die Hände wachsen lassen: Eine Zukunftsinitiative an der Staatlichen Hochschule für Musik und Darstellende Kunst Stuttgart zum Umgang mit pianistischer Vielfalt.* Staatliche Hochschule für Musik und Darstellende Kunst Stuttgart. https://hmdk-stuttgart.de/sites/default/files/2025-02/2024-3_sirius_6.0_-_klaviaturen_die_hande_wachsen_lassen_final_dgfmm.pdf.
[99] Ibid.
[100] "Sirius 6.0 Meets Steinway D on Stage." *Nuremberg University of Music,* https://www.hfm-nuernberg.de/en/news/detail/sirius-60-meets-steinway-d-on-stage. Accessed July 22, 2025.

DS Standard Foundation

The DS Standard Foundation is run by David Steinbuhler and his family. The main focus of the foundation is to provide alternative size keyboards to music schools and other music institutions in an effort to raise awareness and expose a larger group of pianists to the idea. Their lease program to universities has afforded many students the opportunity to gain experience with narrower keyboards. They also continue to make retrofit keyboards for private customers.

The DS Standard Foundation's website includes an abundance of background information and videos about alternatively sized keyboards. Visit their website at https://dsstandardfoundation.org/.

Individual Artists' Websites

Many amateur and professional pianists play and advocate for narrower keyboards. Here's a sampling of artists and their websites where you can read more about their stories and learn how narrower keyboards have helped them. In some cases, the link is to a *YouTube* video or other article in which the artist has specifically discussed and/or demonstrated narrower keyboards.

Tiffany Goff, pianist, composer, and teacher
https://www.tiffanygoff.com/studio
https://www.skinnykeys.com/[101]

Linda Gould, pianist, educator, and co-founder of Narrow Keys
https://www.playpianochordstoday.com/narrow

Carol Leone, Chair of Piano Studies and Professor of Piano at SMU Meadows School of the Arts
http://www.carolleone.com/ergonomic-keyboards/

---

[101] This second site, also maintained by Tiffany Goff, is where she focuses on narrower keyboards. In the video documenting her visit to Titusville, PA to meet David Steinbuhler and try a narrower keyboard for the first time, her emotional reaction to the keyboard is deeply moving. Her experience underscores the personal significance narrower keyboards have on pianists who have been limited by the conventional keyboard size for years or even decades.

Katie O'Rourke, music educator
https://www.pianowithkatie.com/blog/piano-for-small-hands

Hannah Reimann, Professional pianist and founder of Stretto Piano Festivals
https://www.npr.org/2024/05/23/nx-s1-4937937/pianist-seeks-equity-with-narrower-instruments

Susan Tomes, professional pianist
https://www.susantomes.com/blog/piano-keyboards-for-smaller-hands/

Lionel Yu, professional pianist
https://www.youtube.com/watch?v=ZXlknI-Jc48

BIBLIOGRAPHY AND FURTHER READING

"Athena." *Narrow Keys,* https://www.narrowkeys.com/athena. Accessed July 17, 2025.

BBC Four, "Oscar Peterson Interview with André Previn part 5." *YouTube,* uploaded by @another_bites_the_crust_pizzas_uk, February 19, 2008, https://www.youtube.com/watch?v=u2cyoI-mRiw.

Bennett, Arnold. *Sacred and Profane Love.* Project Gutenberg, 2004. https://www.gutenberg.org/files/11360/11360-h/11360-h.htm. Accessed July 18, 2025.

Boyle, R., Boyle, R., and Booker, E. (2015, July). "Pianist Hand Spans: Gender and Ethnic Differences and Implications for Piano Playing." In L. Edwards (Ed.), *Proceedings of the 12th Australasian Piano Pedagogy Conference.* Australasian Piano Pedagogy

Conference Association. https://appca.com.au/allproceedings/179%20PRPaper%20-%20Boyles-Booker.pdf.

Boyle, Rhonda. "The Real Reason Men Dominate Major Piano Competitions." *International Piano,* Autumn 2024.

Donison, Christopher. "DS Keyboard." *Christopher Donison,* http://www.chrisdonison.com/keyboard.html. Accessed July 16, 2025.

"Epidemiological and Clinical Studies." *Pianists for Alternatively Sized Keyboards,* https://paskpiano.org/epidemiological-and-clinical-studies/. Accessed July 15, 2025.

"Fairkey-direct." *ergonomic piano keyboards,* https://www.fairkey.direct/. Accessed July 25, 2025.

Goff, Tiffany. *SkinnyKeys,* https://www.skinnykeys.com/. Accessed September 1, 2025.

"Home." *Kaduk Musical Instruments,* https://www.kaduk.nl/. Accessed July 28, 2025.

"How Many Sizes?" *Pianists for Alternatively Sized Keyboards,* https://paskpiano.org/how-many-sizes/. Accessed July 18, 2025.

"Josef Hofmann – The Pianist Inventor." *Piano Street Magazine,* https://www.pianostreet.com/blog/articles/josef-hofmann-the-pianist-inventor-13049/. Accessed August 19, 2025.

"Josef Hofmann." *Steinway & Sons,* https://www.steinway.com/artists/josef-hofmann. Accessed July 16, 2025.

"Keyboard History." *Pianists for Alternatively Sized Keyboards,* https://paskpiano.org/keyboard-history/. Accessed July 13, 2025.

Leone, Carol. "Ergonomic Keyboards: Size Does Matter." *Piano Professional,* 38 ed., vol. Summer 2015, pp. 32-35.

Leone, Carol. "Goldilocks Had a Choice." *American Music Teacher,* June/July 2003.

Leone, Carol. "A New "Key" to Success: Addressing Pianists' Injuries Through Keyboard Size." *Clavier Companion,* May/June 2014.

Leone, Carol. "Personal Touch: Dr. Carol Leone challenges the orthodoxy of a one-size-fits-all approach to the piano." *International Piano,* http://internationalpiano.com.

Leone, Carol. "Size is Key." *Clavier Companion,* Frances Clark Center for Keyboard Pedagogy, vol. 7, no. 5, pp. 11-21, September/October 2015.

"New Standard for Smaller Piano Keyboards." *LivingPianos*, https://livingpianos.com/standart-smaller-keyboards. Accessed August 19, 2025.

"Overcoming the Barriers." *Pianists for Alternatively Sized Keyboards,* https://paskpiano.org/overcoming-the-barriers/. Accessed July 18, 2025.

"A Piano for Smaller Hands Comes to UdeM." *UdeMNouvelles,* https://nouvelles.umontreal.ca/en/article/2024/04/30/a-piano-for-smaller-hands-comes-to-udem/. Accessed July 18, 2025.

"Resources & links." *Pianists for Alternatively Sized Keyboards,* https://paskpiano.org/resources-and-links/. Accessed July 21, 2025.

"Respons." *Kaduk Musical Instruments,* https://www.kaduk.nl/flagship-projects/respons. Accessed July 28, 2025.

Rogers, Evans. "The Shout Chorus." *Big Band Arranging,* https://www.evanrogersmusic.com/blog-contents/big-band-arranging/the-shout-chorus. Accessed July 14, 2025.

Schwab, C. et al. (2025). "Enthesis Size and Hand Preference: Asymmetry in Humans and Nonhuman Primates." *Scientific Reports,* https://pmc.ncbi.nlm.nih.gov/articles/PMC11922003/. Accessed August 24, 2025.

"Sirius 6.0 Meets Steinway D on Stage." *Nuremberg University of Music,* https://www.hfm-nuernberg.de/en/news/detail/sirius-60-meets-steinway-d-on-stage. Accessed July 22, 2025.

Siskind, Jeremy. *Playing Solo Jazz Piano,* edited by Gail Lew, Jeremy Siskind Music Publishing, 2020.

Steinbuhler, David. "About." *Standard Foundation,* https://dsstandardfoundation.org/about/. Accessed July 17, 2025.

Steinbuhler, David. "The DS Standard." *Standard Foundation,* https://dsstandardfoundation.org/the-standards/#story. Accessed July 16, 2025.

Steinbuhler, David. "Products." *Standard Foundation,* https://dsstandardfoundation.org/products/. Accessed July 17, 2025.

Steinbuhler, David (2000). Reduced-Size Keyboards (U.S. Patent No. 6,118,063). U.S. Patent and Trademark Office.

Steinbuhler, David (1998). Stiffened Key (U.S. Patent No. 5,847,301). U.S. Patent and Trademark Office.

Stöger, M. (February 2024). *SIRIUS 6.0 – Klaviaturen, die Hände wachsen lassen: Eine Zukunftsinitiative an der Staatlichen Hochschule für Musik und Darstellende Kunst Stuttgart zum Umgang mit pianistischer Vielfalt.* Staatliche Hochschule für Musik und Darstellende Kunst Stuttgart. https://hmdk-stuttgart.de/sites/default/files/2025-02/2024-3_sirius_6.0_-_klaviaturen_die_hande_wachsen_lassen_final_dgfmm.pdf.

"Stretto-Piano." *August Förster,* https://www.august-foerster.de/de/stretto-piano/. Accessed August 27, 2025.

Topham, Tim, "The Narrow Key Piano Crusade with Linda Gould and Rhonda Boyle." *YouTube,* uploaded by @TopMusicCo - Tim Topham, December 10, 2023.

"Wippen." *Britannica,* https://www.britannica.com/art/wippen. Accessed August 20, 2025.

Yu, Lionel, "Piano's Darkest Secret." *YouTube,* uploaded by @MusicalBasics, February 5, 2022, https://www.youtube.com/watch?v=ZXlknI-Jc48.

INDEX

www.ingramcontent.com/pod-product-compliance
Lightning Source LLC
Chambersburg PA
CBHW051313120626
46547CB00015B/2215